Sæ-sii Meditation:
How to Find Your Bliss in 15 Minutes a Day

Lorraine Turner

TURNER &
MULLANEY
PUBLISHERS

Praise for Lorraine Turner's *Sæ-Sii Meditation*:

"A wonderful starting point for anyone embarking on a meditative journey. Twenty-five lessons give the reader's explorations a focus and real life examples and samples of personal journal entries help the practitioner better understand the techniques and philosophy being introduced. A fine manual for the beginner and those experienced in meditation alike."
Dana Doerksen, Librarian, Seattle Metaphysical Library

"The word "meditation" can be quite intimidating to many people. Lorraine Turner is a master at simplifying this life skill into something as easy as breathing. She also shows the reader how this method can help overcome difficult situations and even deep personal issues. If you have ever wanted to learn meditation, but thought it would be too difficult, this is a must-read."
Wynter Worsthorne, Animal Communicator, AnimalTalkAfrica

"Lorraine Turner is one of a rare breed of gifted and spiritually aware individuals. Blessed with powerful insight into the tribulations of the human condition and drawing upon her unique life experiences she offers a masterful set of tools through which the route to inner peace and contentment can be found.

Utilizing simple, yet profound techniques that are easy to adapt, the author combines her own insight, knowledge, wisdom and humour to guide the reader on a joyful journey of self-discovery, ultimately leading to bliss.

The modus operandi of Sæ-Sii Meditation is simplicity itself and anyone can follow the pathway so eloquently depicted within these pages. Nothing is required other than the stilled calmness of the mind and our own internal teacher. Indeed, as Lorraine so eloquently states 'Drift into your silence and appreciate that you were given the wisest council on earth….your inner voice.'

Enjoy the journey of a lifetime and prepare to be both seriously inspired and enlightened. You may never be the same again."
Robert Goodwin, Deep Trance Medium

"An amazing read. A true way of finding that genuine peace within. Easy to follow and achieve. Beautifully written."
Bernie Scott, Spiritual Medium

Five-star reviews from readers:

"A wonderful well written guide on how to apply this meditation to your daily life. What Lorraine writes I can so relate to and it makes each lesson mean so much more. It's not just exercises in meditation it's a way to connect to your own spirit and to life around you. Letting go and being your own true self. Thank you for writing this."

"I love the daily "thought" that combines with each meditation. I sometimes do one "thought" two or three days in a row. I have even gone back to a "thought" also when needed. A great guide book."

"I enjoyed reading her style of writing. I also particularly enjoyed her pie chart graph. To me it was worth the price just to get that and consider what's important to me. I'd buy it again and plan to read it again."

"I have read countless books about meditation, nothing comes close to this user friendly guide to what mediation really is and how these little lessons can make a big difference in your life. Lorraine's writing style is like sitting down with a friend having a conversation that stays with you, changes your outlook about yourself, personal environment and the world we live in."

"This book came into my life at the right time. It was at a time of anxiety and stress where I needed to quiet the inner chatter. Meditation has never been easy for me but this book changed my feeling about it. Lorraine Turner explains in 25 simple and clear lessons how to find your inner peace, quiet your mind and stop that pesky inner chatter."

Copyright © 2019 Lorraine Turner. All rights reserved

First print edition, October 2019

Turner and Mullaney, Publishers
CalicoHorses.com

Turner & Mullaney, Publishers is an imprint of The Library of American Comics LLC. All rights reserved. With the exception of brief quotations used for review purposes, none of the contents of this publication may be reprinted without the permission of the publisher. No part of this book may be reproduced or transmitted in any form, electronic or mechanical, including photocopying, recording, or by any information and retrieval system, without permission in writing from the publisher. The characters and events in this book are ficticious. Any similarly to real persons, living or dead, is coincidental and not intended by the author. Printed in the United States.

Thanks and acknowledgments:

To my loving children, who have always inspired and loved me through sunshine and rain.

To my parents, now in spirit, who continue to encourage me to speak out and help others.

To my lifelong friend Suzanne Montgomery, who will always hold a special place in my heart. Thank you for your diligent proofreading of this book.

To the readers and followers who have graciously submitted their meditations to allow readers an insight on how simple it is to just "let go."

To Mick and Sylvie Avery and spirit guide Gregory Haye, who taught me the simple method of Sæ-sii meditation—I am eternally grateful and promise to share this light with those looking to follow their bliss.

And to my best friend and husband Dean Mullaney, who continues to support my endeavors no matter how bizarre they may seem. You have always understood the need to foster self-love in order to blossom, and I am abundantly happy as I wake to daily laughter walking by your side.

I dedicate this book to some of my greatest teachers on Earth,
my three children…
Jake, Jessi, and Jason
Thank you for bringing me such joy.

CONTENTS

8	**Introduction**
14	**Lesson 1: Disconnecting Your Brain**
	The Importance of Reaching a Daydream State
16	**Lesson 2: Meditation Means Letting Go**
	The Art of Not Doing
22	**Lesson 3: Being True to Yourself**
	Trusting Your Inner Voice
25	**Lesson 4: You're Valuable**
	How Are You Measuring Your Self Worth?
29	**Lesson 5: Inundated with Information**
	Who is in Control of Your Decisions?
34	**Lesson 6: Living in the Now**
	How to Release Your Yesterdays
38	**Lesson 7: Mind Shifts**
	Your Ability to Control Your Emotions
43	**Lesson 8: Embrace Awareness**
	Your Parents Aren't You
50	**Lesson 9: Moving Thought Into Action**
	How to Make Your Dreams Come True
54	**Lesson 10: Release the Chatter and Listen Within**
	How to Communicate with Yourself
58	**Lesson 11: Push Your Reset Button**
	It's Okay to Change Your Mind
61	**Lesson 12: Vibrational Check-Ups**
	Tuning Into Your Heart's Song
65	**Lesson 13: Rising Above the Negative Input**
	Tune it Out and Protect Your Energy

69	**Lesson 14: Lessons Our Children Teach Us** *Wise Counsel Comes from All Ages*
73	**Lesson 15: Societally-Conscious Guilt Trips** *Your Opinion is the Only One That Matters*
77	**Lesson 16: Your Journey is Not a Competition** *There is No Enlightenment Certificate*
80	**Lesson 17: Keeper of the Treasure** *Your Experiences are Priceless*
84	**Lesson 18: Toxic Relationship Residue** *How to Remove the "Dis Ease"*
88	**Lesson 19: The Good Odd** *Popular Opinion Doesn't Instill Harmony and Self-Love*
93	**Lesson 20: Smiling Through Broken Glass** *Your Life Experiences Are a Work of Beauty*
96	**Lesson 21: Removing Drama From Trauma** *How to Become More Emotionally Stable*
101	**Interlude—A Time of Reflection** *Sample Meditation Journals From Readers*
108	**Lesson 22: Decreasing Clutter Increases Clarity** *Clearing Away Stuff Brings Coherence*
112	**Lesson 23: Good Vibrations Bring Good Health** *How to Let Your Inner Light Shine*
117	**Lesson 24: People Are Pages** *You Are the Author of Your Life Story*
122	**Lesson 25: The Attitude of Gratitude** *Recognizing the Value of Appreciation*
125	**Guided Meditations**

Introduction

Before we begin…

This book is the result of spending many frustrating hours attempting different methods of meditation until I finally found a model that worked for me. After sharing it with friends and family, and eventually others, I came to see that the art of Sæ-sii meditation is a tool that can benefit a great many people. It's one that you, too, can learn. It's my hope that you will not only discover the key to finding your own inner voice, but that you will then pass that knowledge on to others.

What is Sæ-sii meditation? It's learning to still your chattering mind and erase all surface thoughts. It is something learned gradually as you sit in silence for fifteen minutes daily, training yourself to LET GO of thoughts as living things, and allowing your higher self or the "back-up hard drive" of your mind to come forward.

It is as simple as that.

This is a daily practice. You are not waiting for something to happen. You don't DO anything, for that matter. At first you may only be able to sit for seconds without a thought popping in. Learning to still your chattering mind will become easier each time you try it. Gradually you'll be able to sit without thoughts for minutes at a time. Eventually you will be able to switch off and let go for fifteen minutes.

What lies ahead? The pathway to your bliss.

The lessons in this book are interactive and you will want to prepare yourself by being completely at rest before you begin. Find a comfortable chair in a quiet space. Each lesson begins with a positive affirmation. Read the affirmation and allow these peaceful statements to wash over you as you sit with your eyes closed. Now you're ready to begin.

You will probably need to read this introduction slowly until you get used to the concept. I told you that thoughts are living things and you may be thinking, "Am I reading this correctly?"

Yes, this is one of the most important elements I teach. Your thoughts are THINGS. They affect you and the world around you. Meditation helps you to uncover what role they are playing in your life. Are they bringing you joy—or wreaking havoc? After you have absorbed this important fact you are ready to begin Sæ-sii meditation.

You will use this meditation to disconnect from the outer world and connect to your higher consciousness. *Just taking this simple action of giving yourself fifteen minutes of stillness is a step towards loving yourself and feeling more worthy.*

It isn't always easy, however, to tame that active mind. We can use every excuse we know to avoid getting started. After all, we have chores that need to be done, lists to compile, tasks that require our attention. But we need to remember—we're only talking about fifteen minutes a day. Is any chore so important that it should throw a roadblock in our path to solitude and self-love?

The important thing is to actually start. If your daily "to do" list keeps popping in your head, then begin with only a minute of shut-off time. Stretch it to two minutes, and then five. You'll be surprised at how easy it is to gradually work your way up to fifteen minutes. This beautiful connection with SELF may help you move through your daily life with more purpose and less stress. By making the effort, you are validating your worth. You deserve this.

The importance of a comfortable space...

Before you begin daily Sæ-sii meditation, you will want to prepare yourself by being completely at rest. Please approach your meditation in silence. Find a quiet space in your own home and set it apart as your place to disconnect. You will find it beneficial if you are able to go to this place at the same time each day. Although a garden bench sounds lovely it may not be best suited to all forms of weather. Find a space where you will be undisturbed and uninterrupted. Close the door and turn the lock. Power-off all electronic devices that may beep or ping. Turn off or dim the lights. Find a comfortable chair. You may choose to do this lying down, but keep in mind that this might make you fall asleep and that is not meditation…that's a nap.

No music, aromas, or candles are necessary.

In addition to finding a space for your daily meditations, look for a peaceful place to read this book where you will not be disturbed. There are twenty-five interactive lessons and each one begins with a Mind-Body preparation and a positive affirmation. These are designed to help you find your bliss.

How to begin…

1. Close your eyes, say an invocation asking for protection, and state your intention. This is not a religious prayer; it is simply a statement to the universe asking for a safe passage as you open your mind to a more spiritual awareness. Safe passage into the world of the unknown is very important and allows a corner of your rational thinking brain to feel calm. This is a gateway to letting go of thought. Setting your intention allows you to be clear about what you hope to achieve as you disconnect from your conscious mind. Don't worry about the time as you will set that internal alarm by adding, "I wish to sit for fifteen minutes," and you will be brought back to your fully conscious state in that length of time—no alarms needed. Meditation is much like daydreaming.

Here is an example of the prayer I use:
  To my highest guides and helpers second to none
  Bless me and keep me safe at this time that I sit
  Knowing that all that is said, done and heard, felt or sensed in any way
  is with absolute love as I blend myself with my consciousness
  I wish at this time to be at one with my spirit. (Set your intention, what do you hope to achieve?)
  I would like to return to normal wakefulness in fifteen minutes.

Another example of intent could be:
  I wish at this time to be at peace.
  I wish at this time to be one with the universe.
  I wish at this time to help develop my spiritual gifts.

2. Allow your mind to sit in silence for fifteen minutes.

   At first you may see total blackness and then perhaps some fog or static or just plain old nothing…GOOD. A blank mind is your goal. Thoughts may wander in; of course they will. This is because you are just beginning to learn how to shut them off. Remember that this is your *development phase* and you will be learning this method over a period of time. Each time you do this it's as if invisible computer technicians are fixing the wires and adding the proper coding to access your back-up hard drive.

   A good example is like visiting a beauty salon. You close your eyes and feel them working, and you know they are doing something. Obviously you feel them, but the process is being done TO you as you sit. Or imagine a doctor's visit as they are looking into your ears or throat and you are simply following instructions. This examination is being done TO you as you sit. If these people were invisible and you could not necessarily feel them working on you…that's exactly how to imagine what is being accomplished when we rest our minds for fifteen minutes. Just think of all of these beings as your guides and helpers. All of the necessary work to connect your mind to your higher self is being brought TO you as you sit in silence. That's all there is to it.

This daily meditation is your linking-up time. You are not waiting for or doing anything. You are simply sitting in silence and allowing your ability to NOT THINK happen in order to have a clean slate for information to be brought TO you. Moments of inspiring thought may not occur DURING the meditation, but instead while you are performing an ordinary household chore, driving your car, or walking your dog. Bam! It hits you—some remarkable realization reveals itself and you are almost giddy with excitement. But it all starts with daily meditation.

Once you have this inspiration, you'll want to do something with it. This is the only DOING part of the meditation. Following this nugget of inspiring thought and actually creating with it is up to you. How? By understanding that you have had this ability all along and that perhaps negativity, self-doubt, or just time management has kept you from bringing it to fruition. Meditation helped unlock it and brought it to you. This is just one of the reasons why you meditate. The rewards are never-ending and too long to list.

Each time you sit in silence, relax and let go. Every time a thought creeps in, just pull your mind away from it. Not giving energy to the thought will allow it to melt away. Over time you will begin to see that you have trained your mind to shut off this thinking. Let me give you an example:

You are busy working on a project and you have a deadline. All is going well and you get a phone call from a family member who wants to come for a future visit. You chat and promise to call them back and disconnect…but do you really? If you are like

most people you will begin to think of this event. Where will they sleep? Do they have special dietary needs? What will they require for entertainment? This list is endless and suddenly you stop and say, "I will not think of this because I need to finish my project. I can think of this later." POOF. Your meditation has given you this skill to filter which thoughts are welcome at any given time. It's as easy as that.
3. When closing a meditation always say thank you to the universe and all of the guides and helpers that were just with you. It does not matter if you believe in guides or helpers (I didn't until incredible insight was given)—just remember to finish with gratitude.

Lesson 1:

Disconnecting Your Brain—
The Importance of Reaching a Daydream State

Mind/Body Preparation: *Let us begin by taking three deep, cleansing breaths. Breathe in slowly and exhale slowly. Each time you exhale, relax deeper into your seat. Unclench your jaw and relax all of your muscles. As you exhale take this thought with you before closing your eyes and sitting for a few moments in silence: "I can disconnect."*

• • • • •

Meditation clears a space for our higher conscious to communicate with us.

Although I do not consider myself a science expert, I learned about the mechanism of the brain in order to help me better understand meditation. Our brain has four different types of waves, occurring while you're thinking, concentrating on what you are doing, sleeping, or dreaming. They are called beta, alpha, theta, and delta. These waves come in cycles and are measured per second. Scientists can record brain activity by attaching electrodes to the scalp and connecting these electrodes to a machine called an "electroencephalograph." Why learn about these brain waves and what do they have to do with meditation? Hopefully by absorbing some of this information you will be able to better recognize the condition of un-hooking conscious thoughts in order to enjoy the benefits of zoning out.

Brain Wave States
  Beta: Fully Conscious/Awake…BUSY, BUSY, BUSY thinking
  Alpha: Light Sleep/Dreams/Meditation/Creative Visualization/ Connection to the Subconscious

Theta: Deep Sleep/Lucid Dreaming/Deep Trance/Deep Hypnosis
Delta: Very Deep Sleep/Unconscious State

When we meditate we are trying to achieve Alpha state. This is a place where you are not fully awake and yet not fully asleep. The best way to describe this is when you are just beginning to stir in the morning and your eyes have not opened and you are halfway between slumber and wakefulness. For me it usually happens between 4AM and 6AM. Your schedule may be different. This is an excellent time to begin a meditation.

Each time you sit in your quiet space and relax away all thoughts, you will be drifting into a daydream state. It is exactly like driving your car and arriving safely at your destination without paying attention to the places along the way. Many people use meditation to improve their athletic abilities, creativity, and overall health. How? By understanding that your mind can LET GO and move away from the busy thoughts and relax into a cloud of silence. This helps you disconnect from patterns of thought that could become roadblocks.

You don't need to become a science wizard to understand meditation. Achieving Alpha state comes with practice and is developed over time.

Lesson 2:

Meditation Means Letting Go—
The Art of Not Doing

Mind/Body Preparation: *Quietly focus on your breathing. Now take three deep, cleansing breaths. Breathing in through your nose and out through your mouth. This is called circle breathing. Relax deep down into your comfy chair and before closing your eyes allow the following thought to slowly tumble down from the crown of your head, water-falling across your body and onto the floor: "My journey begins today."*

• • • • •

Meditation helps us to instantly escape to a place where we can relax into inner peace.

Meditation is one of the best ways to instill inner peace and self-love. Achieving this is a wonderful goal for anyone and my purpose for writing this book. If you were to explore all other types of meditation you would find that visual cues such as those found in videos and audio instructional formats are quite common. They usually start off with instructions such as, "Imagine you are walking down a path."

Personally, no matter how hard I tried, I never saw a path…or a garden or a door or anything else. So why do some people have success with those methods and others not? Everyone is wired differently and no two people will be able to meditate exactly the same way. I teach a silent meditation because it allows you to switch off any time anywhere. Let me give some examples of when it can be useful:

- Someone nearby is talking non-stop on a cell phone
- A heated argument breaks out next to you
- You're stuck in a dentist's office waiting room

Can you see how difficult it would be to begin a meditation to remove yourself mentally from the situation if you had to first play a certain song, or listen to a specific voice instructor, or use incense or other material items? By learning to do this in complete silence you can find that peaceful state wherever you are.

When I first began meditation I was intrigued by the vivid, almost surreal experiences that were depicted in various books and videos. Wow, I thought, how could this be? I studied books, researched online, watched YouTube how-to videos, and even attended an exclusive workshop to learn how to "do it."

If you read some of the claims made by others you will probably respond much like I did.

"Why can't I do this? Am I doing it wrong? Others seem to have amazing mind-blowing experiences…but I just sit here thinking of the laundry or the traffic sounds outside my window."

Meditation is a time of letting go of all thought. It takes practice and it takes patience. If you can remember back to simple tasks that you once learned and can now do effortlessly, you will understand this meaning. Photography—you used to cut off all the heads. Cooking—you used to either serve food undercooked or scorched. Computer—you needed a child to teach you.

That's when I discovered that meditation isn't about seeing or experiencing surreal things—it's about NOT doing. You simply find yourself a quiet haven, relax, and float into nothingness. Sure, thoughts can slip in and you may even scold yourself, "I need to stop thinking about the day's events!" But no scolding necessary. Each time you begin and a thought comes fluttering in, learn to pay it ZERO attention and it will vanish. In time you will be able to do this effortlessly.

Approach your meditation with a feeling of simplicity. This is not about achieving anything that others may have told you about or that you may have read. This is YOUR experience and this is your personal journey. You are closing your eyes and attuning yourself to your beautiful spirit who is with you always. Learning to release all thought allows your higher consciousness to connect with you. You are opening a door that has always been there. This connection does not necessarily come at the time you are in meditation. You may find yourself a few hours later or even the next day in a moment of realization. A sparkle of inspiration awakes within you—it just suddenly appears as if out of the blue. And here you thought you were just sitting in silence and nothing "happened." The happening may not be something you are able to put into words…but it is occurring nonetheless.

Doing nothing was the hardest part for me. I am an active person and a multi-tasker, constantly juggling projects. Sitting in total silence and NOT waiting for something to happen…well, it took months to finally really "let go" of all thoughts. This is an ongoing process and we progress at our own pace, so stay with it. If you only gain seconds of "letting go," it is perfectly normal. It will get easier and you will be able to sit for longer spans as you learn to switch-off and float. Those seconds will turn into minutes and soon you will be silent for fifteen minutes daily and the rewards will be life changing.

One of the ways to help you monitor your progress is to keep a journal. Recording your progress and jotting down notes will give you clues to how communication with your higher self is proceeding. Write EVERYTHING you see, hear, think, smell, and sense. I repeat …WRITE EVERYTHING. You will be able to glean extraordinary information about YOU once you have collected a journal and are able to look back on it for comparison. This is a priceless tool and it's a key to unlocking the treasures of your mind. I personally use a computer text-editing program daily so I can look up similar words or situations. Some prefer to hand write them, but this can become difficult when you are searching for a subject or word that appeared to you months ago. Here are few examples of some of my earliest notes. I am a graphic designer and as you will see my meditations often bring me artistic inspiration.

• • • • •

Journal Notes

November 19: My daily meditations of 15 minutes of letting go and facing silence is very hard for me. I just sit there frustrated and finally get up. I ask for protection, I specifically talk to my guides, but I am just alone in my head trying not to chatter.

It has been bothering me. I have stayed with it, but to be honest I want to give up. I know it takes time and I am just being my impatient self, but it really is a pain.

January 2: Meditation is bringing me knowledge and peace.

I believe this daily exercise of letting go is allowing me to have a deeper understanding of what my inner voice seems to reveal to me. I suppose it's all in the way we look at it. To some it would seem I am sitting in a room in silence, no communication at all, or maybe I am building and developing a tool that will help unite with my spirit. I choose to think I am in my work-in-progress-mode.

I am finally realizing that the "timing" it takes to reach Alpha state is unique to each of us. Priceless.

February 4: Background: I am stuck on the cover for a Flash Gordon archival book I am working on. I was getting there, sort of close…but no go. I told myself I would revisit the project tomorrow when I was fresh. I called it a night and shut down my computer.

4:00 AM: I stir and decide to meditate as I am not completely awake (Alpha state) and I decide to just enjoy the silence of my mind and accept whatever message comes. A thought—"Constellation"—comes to me.

Huh? Constellation?

Now the thought becomes "Star charts… use the universe."

I am not really paying attention as I let my mind just float, and then a male voice says, "Look up Chester Winfield."

Now my attention is all tuned in. Male voices, names...stars? I thank my guides and think upon what just happened slowly filtering through. Oh man...the missing element in my Flash Gordon cover! I go to the computer and proceed to look for galaxy photos that I can purchase and use as an element for my background. It sings! (Still searching for Chester Winfield.)

April 16: I see blackness. All is silent. I finish my meditation and feel rejuvenated and give thanks.

August 3: I asked guides to help me discover the purpose of my spiritual gifts—what are they and how should I use them to benefit others?

A bright swirling light appears and it brings a message. "You are a messenger—You are to write, speak, teach and deliver the message—do not worry about your material needs—all will be met—just go forth and deliver—this is your greatest gift... you are a communicator."

October 14: I saw a door with black-and-white headshot photos appearing. As each one came into view it would pause and then vanish and another took its place. This happened about ten times and I saw my Uncle Harry's photo and then it ended. Oh, how I miss him, how wonderful to see him again!

November 19: I felt that I had a meeting with my guides. Many were seated and speaking. I am to teach Awareness through Art. Their message was very strong that it should be about nature and our planet.

December 8: I sit in silence. I drift and float into nothingness. I smell cinnamon. I finish and feel such renewed energy and give thanks.

• • • • •

As you can see, my journals cover many subject matters and only have meaning for me. They're like tiny puzzle pieces that may fit together over time. Yours will be filled with YOUR awareness and perhaps may startle you, as they can seem bizarre and quite extraordinary...

Welcome to your journey!

Sæ-sii meditation is a process and in the beginning you may feel it is utterly pointless. It isn't. It may take days, weeks, or months of repeating this fifteen-minute daily practice of "letting go" of all thought. One day you will find yourself in a powerful state of self-love and all of those daily meditations will reveal their value. This increases self-worth. Connecting with your beautiful spirit helps bring this to the surface. As you begin to understand this dynamic tool that is available to all, you will find it contagiously spreading to the world around you...to your family, pets, community, nature, and the planet. This is the "doing" part of meditation. It is how you go forth and it begins with making the connection to the beautiful YOU within. Sæ-sii meditation can open that door.

Lesson 3:

Being True to Yourself—
Trusting Your Inner Voice

Mind/Body Preparation: *Find a comfy place and quiet your mind. Release all tension. Take a deep cleansing breath and let all thoughts dissipate. Just take a few moments to pause, sitting in silence, and before closing your eyes ask yourself this simple question: "Am I being true to myself?"*

•••••

Am I being—indicates action

True—opposite of false

To myself—does not denote anyone else

Meditation can unravel the root of thoughts. Where did they originate and are they beneficial? Learning to weed out unhealthy thoughts can lead us closer to finding our bliss.

This simple question can help bring realization to matters that appear to be repeated patterns in your life. Your thoughts and beliefs may actually have been formed by the opinions of others, not by who and what you really are. After all, who knows us better than ourselves?

We can look at the simplest of things in our lives.
- Job or career
- Foods we purchase
- Media and entertainment choices
- How we raise our children
- How we create, in the home, garden, etc.

By asking yourself this question you will learn to make better choices in your life. These choices may apply to relationships, who you allow into your inner circle, your belief systems…whether you are going along with the pack or if you need to strike out on your own.

When faced with a choice and by asking, "Am I being true to myself?", you may find yourself arguing with your inner voice. If it has to do with a relationship, you might hear, "But we have so much fun together, we have a lot in common, his (her) conversations challenge me, and he's (she's) pretty darn good looking!"

But does this really mean you should give up your apartment and move in together? Be honest—do you enjoy your alone time, the stillness of your personal space, following your own schedule, career path, etc.? If you can continue doing what makes you happy and also share your space, then you are making a choice based on being true to yourself. If not, recognize that within this compromise, part of you has just paid a price. In order to live with someone else, you have given up something which brings you joy deep within. Can you have both? Yes, it is absolutely possible. You can create an environment where you have mutual respect in allowing each other to have their own space and understand that in order to love themself they too have to be true to who they are.

There are times when you may find yourself going along with someone else's plan that makes you uncomfortable.
- Watching entertainment you don't enjoy
- Doing something unscrupulous in the workplace
- Remaining silent as a racist expounds views with which you disagree
- Submitting to a pushy salesman

If you allow yourself to be swept into the arena of "this just doesn't feel right," you need to remove yourself as quickly as possible. Your inner voice is sending you red flares—upset stomach, dry mouth, headaches, and your feet feel as if they have cinder blocks attached to them; they're not moving! Use the tools given to you through meditation to SHIFT to a space that feels right.

Do not let your mind get sidetracked by the "what ifs." You need to move your mind away from these minefields that may cause you to engage in something that is contrary to who you are. The "what ifs" are thoughts such as:

- If I don't go they will be disappointed in me
- If I don't buy it they will not reach their goal
- If I don't laugh at their dirty joke they will not like me

How do you navigate away from these "what ifs" and into a place where you can be comfortable in your decision? Recognize that in order to live a life that is truly harmonic, you must begin to understand that only YOU know what it takes to tune into your true self. You know when it "feels right" and you definitely know when it "feels wrong." Trust those feelings and pay attention to them.

It's okay to disappoint others, it's perfectly fine to agree to disagree, and it's okay to say no. Hasn't anyone ever said "No" to you? And when you think back you will find that the world kept spinning and the sun still came up shining the next day. This is not about being true to others; it is about taking a stand and being true to yourself. If you do this, you will not walk with regret but you will skip along your path and enjoy the scenery. Others will have their opinions, naturally, but always keep in mind those are THEIR thoughts, not yours. Begin to accept that you are the one in control of your life. Say yes or say no—but let it be YOUR decision. You will no longer be tip-toeing along in doubt as you face those "what ifs." You will be able to look them straight in the eye because you have already measured it with your "Am I being true to myself?" meter and that meter is happily responding, "YES I AM!"

Lesson 4:

You're Valuable—
How Are You Measuring Your Self Worth?

Mind/Body Preparation: *Before reading this next lesson take a nice long stretch. Roll your shoulders and relax all muscles. Now sink into your comfy reading space. Allow your mind to become still. Relax every part by taking a cleansing breath and removing all tension. Before closing your eyes allow your mind to accept this truth: "Thoughts are living things."*

• • • • •

Meditation can help you shed expectations imposed on you by others and reveal your true self worth.

Early in life each of us has learned that we have these things called thoughts. No one hears them or sees them but they exist. We can think positive or negative thoughts about all aspects of our lives. A parent tells a child to do something and the child sends the thought back, "Not now. I'm having too much fun." When you think a thought it goes out into the universe and it lingers. Your thoughts can attach themselves to you or others. Imagine these thoughts as a sheer, weightless fabric that cloaks you. You have been dressed in these thoughts all of your life. They are a living part of you and there are many, many layers of them.

Look around you at the people who come in all shapes, colors, and sizes. Just like plants, animals, minerals, and elements, we have many varieties. What are your thoughts toward these various people who are sharing your space? Can you look upon them and see their true beauty? Or are you looking at what you have been taught to think of as beautiful. As you people watch, you may be thinking—her nose is too big, his clothes are odd, her skin is not the right color, or he bites his nails, how disgusting. By sending out these thoughts you are placing them into the universe where eventually they will land. Your thoughts will pop up unexpectedly and the opinions you quietly held within your head will escape through your spoken words. Your simple thought blends with theirs and without realizing it you have made someone feel inadequate. Thoughts cling like static material and they now have another negative thought to add to their wardrobe. Imagine a wispy orange sheer fabric now worn over their shoulders along with the countless other colored thoughts they have accumulated over time. This happens without you even being aware as you go along your merry way. The person you sent your orange cloth to now wears it, assured that they were correct in their low opinion of themselves.

Now let's begin to take a closer look at ourselves. We too have many colored weightless thoughts that adorn us. If you were asked to find flaws about your appearance, how would you answer? Some of the replies may be: my feet are too wide, my stomach sticks out, my hair is frizzy, or I'm too short. And if you were allowed to ponder too long, you would probably come up with an itemized list.

These negative thoughts collected over the years can weigh you down and hold you back. Let those thoughts of poor self-image be recognized for what they are. Did they originate in society or popular opinion? Did you begin to wear these layers of unhappy views when someone else laid their perception over you—much like a veil covering up your beautiful self? It's time to discard them now…today and forever!

Let's think of someone you know who can light up a room just by entering it. See them in your mind's eye and say their name to yourself. The energy changes—oh, how you just enjoy their company. You find yourself grinning because you are so happy to be in their presence and you are quite eager to connect. You can actually feel the shift of energy in the room. Did you for one instant say to yourself, "Oh, but their ears are too big, their skin is full of blemishes," or any other ridiculous thoughts? No, of course you didn't…they're beautiful and so are you.

Remember, you are a part of this planet. You are connected to every bird, leaf, and drop of rain. We are all beautiful. Stop allowing yourself and others to rob you of what you truly know deep down inside. DNA and genetics play a huge part in your physical makeup, but it is just a vessel. The you living within is ALL that really matters. If you hold an opinion that you are overweight, for example, are you being honest in your approach? In other words, stop repeating these thoughts, as they will continue to hold you down. These thoughts, which are living things, are being repeated over and over to yourself. They are not only causing you to think less of yourself but are destroying the beautiful you inside. That radiance needs to find its way out so that YOU will light up a room.

How can you stop repeating these negative thoughts that you are wrapping yourself in like a mummy? By relaxing your mind and seeing it for what it is. The thought comes in, you recognize it as a harmful intruder and you pay it ZERO attention. You will practice this over and over each time it flutters in. You will become so good at ignoring this thought that after a while it will come strolling in and you will either laugh at it or tell it, NICE TRY! Sæ-sii meditation can give you this ability.

We are all on a journey. We interact with others and this can cause both positive and negative effects. It is your duty in caring for yourself to recognize these thoughts as living things and stop allowing them to attach themselves to you. You have the power to remove them entirely. Learn to pay less attention to them and replace them with inspiring truthful thoughts. You came into this world as a beautiful spirit…and you still are.

You are capable of using your mind for more than you realize. Like a balloon that is tethered, you need to cut these impressions that hold you down and FLY. Soar up high and take a good look around from this spectacular view. The world looks brighter from up here, your vision looks upon nature and your surroundings in a whole new way. Hmm, those wasp nests near your home suddenly look incredible. You find yourself wondering how long it took to make them. Wow, those insects are like tiny sculptors…who knew? By allowing yourself to connect with the splendor of the world you live in, you can begin to see yourself in a new light.

Learning to assess your value will enable you to examine your thoughts about others, your pets, your family, the environment, and the entire planet. You will be able to send out positive energy, keeping in mind that thoughts are living things. In addition to helping others look differently at themselves, they in turn will see who YOU really are. You are a beautiful person who is filled with self-love.

Lesson 5:

Inundated with Information—
Who is in Control of Your Decisions?

Mind/Body Preparation: *Begin this lesson by allowing all distractions to disappear. Any thought that dances in, pay it no attention. Take a cleansing breath and exhale all tension and allow the tiny dust particles of thought to blow away. Now allow an idea to come to you: "I can choose for myself."*

• • • • •

Meditation can improve the choices you are making. For example, by the simple choice to read this book, you are learning about your internal teacher who gives the best advice of all.

If you were to browse bookstores you would see rows and rows of self-help books. If you were to ask your family and friends for the best way to proceed on any given action they would fill your ears with lots of advice. This advice is their opinion, which they will gladly heap upon you. You can take all of this information and realize that somewhere in this huge pile of data is an answer, but where? To this heap you can add more facts from the media and watch the mountain grow. It becomes enormous and looms before you. But I only need to make a decision about _____ (you fill in the blank). Where or how do I begin?

There are times in your life when you will be called upon to make a serious choice. This can be very frightening. And we may, in fact, give up our right to choose in order to avoid having to make a decision. In doing this, it's as if you have opened the vault and allowed someone else to rob you of your destiny—your path.

Sometimes our choices bring regret. I have had a few of those experiences myself. I remember being invited out to dinner by a co-worker. I was new in town and looked forward to meeting people. As I sat down and glanced at the menu prices, my stomach suddenly became ill. I could barely afford an appetizer, let alone an entrée. I ordered a small salad and water and tried to enjoy the evening. The group chose to split the bill, including the bar tab. I felt I had no choice but to pay an exorbitant price for fear of what my co-worker would think. The evening I had looked forward to was ruined by my inability to speak out. I thought I made a choice to make new friends, not clean out my purse!

So how do you make important decisions? One way is to examine your inner voice. Sæ-sii meditation allows us to turn up the volume. What is it telling you? There is a great tool that can help you speak with your true self. I developed this over a cup of coffee one morning and I call it "The Pie Chart of Life."

How To Use The Pie Chart of Life

Think of any decision you may face—perhaps it's about an important purchase, a health issue, choosing a job, or even a move from your community. Begin to list all of the reasons why you are making it or why you shouldn't. Then imagine an empty circle in your mind (see diagrams) and begin to think of the reasons as pie slices. Create them in size by their importance. Place the most important reasons first and watch the graph develop. Here is an example of my own and how it can be applied.

We were in the process of selling my partner's home in the Florida Keys. It was a beautiful, spacious house on a canal and looked out on open shimmering water. It was a very quiet place sitting at the end of a road and its neighbor was a wide-open protected bird sanctuary. The house had three bedrooms, three bathrooms…and we were two people and a cat. I had just moved in with him and felt homesick for my tiny one bedroom apartment nestled in the funky town of Key West. The island resort was so small that I had sold my car and rode my bike as the only means of transportation. Now that I lived several Keys up the island chain, I had to commute forty minutes by car. I loved Key West's position on the map…FAR AWAY FROM EVERYONE…well most everyone, aside from the tourists that come for the sun, snorkeling, to get drunk, or shop for souvenirs.

As we were discussing where we would live after the sale of his home, we tossed around various options. It was then that we invented the "Pie Chart Of Life" and saw how it could make life easier.

We started to define everything we wanted in a living space. Where could we move that would reflect what we viewed as a place of harmony? We put value on the things that would go into our chart.

- Bike-riding as a mode of transportation
- Close to the beach
- Privacy
- An outdoor area
- A quiet place to do art
- Affordable housing

Bike-riding seemed to loom large for each of us and we wanted to rid ourselves of the daily commute by car to our office. Although Key West is a beautiful town filled with lush nature, it can be very noisy. The rental price of the apartment we were considering would double the cost of our housing expenses. The real estate market was not very good and we may have waited years waiting for someone to buy his home. Were we really willing to risk paying for a mortgage AND a rental apartment just to ride our bikes to work and be closer to a beach? We were assigning a greater importance to the wrong areas. Once we entered all of these elements into the graph, the decision that was nagging us daily was made so easily when we applied The Pie Chart of Life method.

All of the things we both wanted already existed in this beautiful home. We opted to make one of the rooms an office and no longer faced a thirty-mile commute. There were mental adjustments regarding

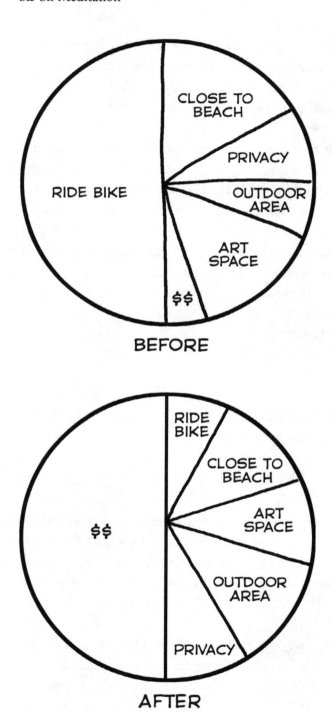

simple things like riding our bikes and a longer trek to the beach. Once we looked at The Pie Chart of Life, we saw that it really wasn't worth moving to a pricey living space in Key West. Together we felt at peace with our decision to remove the home from the real estate market.

Now think of your own example. Think of a decision you need to make that you have been mulling over. Imagine an empty circle and start to list the reasons for making your decision. Fill up your circle. Look at the various shapes and sizes of the pie wedges. Can you begin to see how your mind has known all along how it perceives the direction you should take?

By using this mental tool you will be able to smile at all of the worldly advice and look within for your answers. Those answers are there, just waiting for you to connect to them. This is something that can easily be taught to children as well. This simple method will make a significant difference in your approach to major choices in life—deciding on a vacation destination, choosing a doctor, purchasing a car, furthering your education, or even how to improve your living space. The possibilities are endless.

In the world around us there is a form of mind pollution that can muddy the waters when trying to pick a path. By quieting your mind and stilling your thoughts you can connect with the voice that is always with you. It will take practice to direct your attention away from the noise and jabbering of world opinion and friendly advice. Begin to trust that you know what is best for yourself and enjoy the confidence it brings. You can gain control of your destiny—you only have to listen to yourself.

Lesson 6:

Living in the Now—
How to Release Your Yesterdays

Mind/Body Preparation: *Quiet your mind and relax all thoughts away. Take a few cleansing breaths and release all tension. Do a body scan and look for any signs of tension. From head to toe relax each part of your body. Release any stress, then settle deeper into your chair. Before closing your eyes surround yourself in this thought: "Today is my now."*

•••••

Meditation can bring liberation from thoughts that keep holding you back.

We live in a society where most of us are guided by the hierarchy we were born into. In our development these guides can be parents, guardians, church leaders, schoolteachers, athletic coaches, and our peers. Some of us go through our earliest years much like little soldiers, following whatever the orders of the day were. We learned quickly that marching out of step brought a disapproving or disappointing response. If we held onto those thoughts—keeping in mind that thoughts are living things—then a seed of negativity was planted. We felt compelled to continue on the path that others approved or we would face negative retribution and possible alienation. In reality, we are the ones who place this on ourselves. We choose to allow the thoughts of others to override our own.

This cycle continues throughout our lives. In order to get off this merry-go-round of negativity we must learn to live in the now. The thoughts that others placed on you are weighing you down. Their opinions can swallow your thoughts. They can also infiltrate themselves into your life and spread like a cancer, leaving you filled with doubt…

. "Oh, why did I ever think I could do that?" Now is the time to let them go. This, for some people, is one of the hardest lessons to learn simply because it requires looking deeply within and taking action. It requires being honest with yourself. The action required of you is to STOP THINKING about yesterday.

As you progress in your meditation you will learn to recognize the origin of thought. For example, if someone told you that you could never move into a rural environment because you have always lived in a big city, you may miss a beautiful experience. It was waiting for just the right moment to reveal itself to you alone.

If you were told you couldn't learn to play an instrument because you're not musically talented, you have probably told yourself why bother putting your energy into something which is pointless. But if you ignored that thought of "you can't," you would find, like many skills, all it takes is desire, practice, and commitment to yourself.

If you were taught, "It's too late to go back to school, you missed your chance," you may rob yourself of the riches that education brings. The interaction of like-minded people learning at their own pace and exchanging ideas is something no teacher can put a grade on. This is priceless.

Perhaps you have lived through an emotional trauma—a break up of a relationship, an illness, maybe the loss of a loved one. Yes, this can have lasting effects and I do not make light of the long-term process of healing. If you continue to center your attention on the trauma then you will be rooted in yesterday. In time you may come to learn that by bringing attention to a painful experience only keeps you reliving it over and over again. This is not doing you any good; in fact it is what is stopping you from moving forward. The event was then and this is NOW. You can learn to let go of this through meditation. It takes practice but you will be amazed at the results of this simple daily tool. You will actually feel comforted as if someone has just given you their utmost attention – and they did. That person was you.

Can you think of a situation in your own life when someone else's thought became a roadblock to you?

Years ago, while attending art school, I desperately wanted to become a children's book illustrator. It was my lifelong dream. I began with pen and ink drawings. I studied books in the library and started to develop my own style of watercolor. I practiced and practiced and even followed the path of the artist Beatrix Potter, my muse, and bought mice that I kept in an aquarium in my art studio. I drew them in every position imaginable. I began to interact with these creatures and found myself daydreaming about what it was like to be a mouse. Um…yeah. I was doing everything to move toward my goal of becoming a children's book illustrator. And then one day I met with a woman who represented artists in the children's publishing field. Her advice was this: "You are wearing too many hats. Your work is beautiful, Lorraine, but you must decide what you want to specialize in. You cannot do it all so pick a form of art and stay with it. I can find you work, but in truth you MUST MOVE TO NEW YORK."

Huh—move to New York? How was I supposed to uproot my children and move to a place I knew nothing about in order to fulfill my goal? I was crushed. I stopped trying to pursue this and fell into a deep depression. But twenty-four years later I published my first young readers book, *Calico Horses and the Patchwork Trail*, and guess what… I never moved to New York! I had to learn to STOP THINKING of what this expert told me and follow my gut. Meditation clears away the mental debris that holds you back. Better late than never!

Close you eyes and quiet your mind. Breathe slowly in through your nose and out through your mouth. Just let the cares of the world drift away. Begin to settle your mind into new possibilities that await you and the mysteries that lie asleep. Give yourself permission to release all thoughts of "I can't" and focus your attention on what you CAN do. Remember, the best way to get a thought to dissipate is to not give it any attention. If a negative thought flutters into your focus, simply ignore it. As you practice Sæ-sii meditation daily those thoughts will eventually cease.

You will begin to look ahead with a new attitude. Others will continue to voice their good intentions and advice, but you will be able to identify foreign thoughts as belonging to them, not you—allowing you to continue happily on your journey. Treasures ready to be uncovered are now within your grasp. You will have a life filled with purpose when you move aside the vines and weeds of doubt and start walking in confidence of who YOU truly are.

In doing this others will be attracted to you and they will want to know your secret. By sharing this with your loved ones, especially your little ones, you will actually begin to feel the positive energy flowing all around you. You will be able to take this beautiful loving energy and let it loose on your personal space. It will have a glorious effect on your surroundings as it begins to send a positive message to the people, plants, animals, and universe in which you live. It is a contagious energy that others spend their entire existence seeking. This magnificent energy is available to all people.

Let go of ALL past events, experiences, advice, and misguided journeys, and live in the now. Sometimes we cling to past misfortune as an excuse for our inability to move forward. All pity parties must come to an end. You can move away from these thoughts, as you will clearly see that they are keeping you from living in the now.

Negative attracts negative just as positive attracts positive. Our world needs less negative energy so it can begin to find new ways of healing. Begin to accept that you no longer have to carry the ills of yesterday. They were then…this is NOW! Sleep in peace, knowing as you wake up tomorrow you will hear yourself say, "Hello, world. What can I do today?"

Lesson 7:

Mind Shifts—
Your Ability to Control Your Emotions

Mind/Body Preparation: *Unclench your jaw, your fists, and any areas of tension. Breathe deeply and take a few cleansing breaths. Breathe in all of the beautiful energy of nature and now exhale all the noise and clutter in your head. Float along this current of nothingness. Before closing your eyes allow a simple thought to enter in: "I can shift my mind to a better place."*

• • • • •

Meditation can help you strengthen your ability to "switch off" from negative energy.

The planet around us is struggling to survive. Global warming, sudden shifts in the earth, and catastrophic weather patterns are all bringing their attention to us in a very loud way. "Wake up!" they seem to shout. "Stop ignoring your environment. We are all connected. If we are hurting, then you are suffering too."

We live in an age of technology that has connected our world in a way that no previous generation has ever seen. This communication can work both for and against us. It can bring encouragement and truthful insight or it can lead to utter chaos. We all like to think of ourselves as strong, knowledgeable individuals, and many are, but some people will follow a fool off a cliff. The only way to actually be led by such a fool is to ignore your inner voice and allow others to think for you.

For example, if we know that a storm is coming and are able to use technology to "best guess" its course, we should be able to decide for ourselves (unless we are relying on others because of mental or medical impairments) what the best plan of action should be. Many, many people throughout the ages have lived with the threats of hazardous weather, as well as the pets and wildlife that have gone before us. Did they have the Weather Channel, Facebook, or CNN? No, they simply took the warnings they were given, made the necessary precautions, and gathered with friends and family to wait out the storm. Many had to leave their homes to find a safe haven and some returned to find their dwellings demolished. We live with unforeseen natural environmental events that will continue long after we pass.

No one is advocating that we do not heed a warning. But there must come a time when we listen to our inner voice and separate the real message from the chatter. We need to "tune out" the hype, because that is what it is. In actual fact it sells advertisements. STAY TUNED… BREAKING NEWS…THIS JUST IN. If you step aside and see how it is commercially packaged and delivered, you will recognize it for what it is—sheer drama that instills fear to make you come back for more. The music, the lighting, the flashing scroll of red text, the newsman strapped to a tree…none very helpful in preparing a community. You want to be able to rely on calm, rational decisions and not whipped-up emotional reactions. This is when a Mind Shift is needed most. If you were trying to assist your children or elderly loved ones, how would you approach them—with careful and purposeful direction to lead them to safety—or getting them hyped up over continued fear-inducing updates?

A Mind Shift is a powerful yet simple concept. Instead of allowing yourself to get wrapped up in and follow a negative or useless train of thought, move your mind to a positive and useful course of action.

There are many opportunities to practice this handy Mind Shift tool and if we wanted to we each could probably fill pages and pages creating a list. Think of some events that you encounter in your daily lives in which you have no control. For example (and I will only name a few as they can bring you down emotionally just listing them!):

- Airport hell
- Doctor's office visit…the inner waiting room
- Traffic jams
- Unexpected weather…cancellations and loss of power
- Trip to the Motor Vehicle office

As we look at these examples we can feel the groans as they drag themselves through our lips. Now place yourself in one of these circumstances. For example, you arrive at the Motor Vehicle office and you pull the number 63 and a voice calls out "number 31." You look around and notice the bleak faces…the room is painted gray and actually looks as if it is getting grayer. But you need this document today and you have to wait. Others grumble, some start talking on their phones, and you can feel the air thicken with negativity. It hovers about you like a cloud.

By quieting yourself and breathing easily you can allow your mind to shift. You have complete control of your thoughts. Perhaps you were meant to learn something or maybe you were meant to use this very moment to understand that you have power over your own emotions. This is YOUR journey and you do not have to get swept along with all of the angry emotions of the people around you. Can you sit and see how unique you are—not better than others—no, just able to distance yourself enough to think upon positive things. Shift your attention and focus on a happy place. Maybe it's a loved one, a good book, or a project you need to work out in your mind before you begin to create it.

This ability to shift your mind can remove unnecessary stress in your life. This skill can also help when you sense yourself spinning out of control. If you begin to feel yourself stiffen when a disagreement with someone is about to surface, catch yourself and say, "Mind Shift." Then ask yourself: Is this really how I want to respond? Am I prepared to allow all negative emotional energy to have its free reign? What will this accomplish?

Learn to use this Mind Shift as a lifeboat giving you safe passage to the calmness in which you thrive. When anger is all around you, don't allow yourself to be carried into the debris of negative thoughts. If this means turning off a computer or hanging up the phone, then DO it. This especially means you will need to mentally turn OFF the media (which can be a challenge when it blasts throughout stores, airports, and public places). Mentally tune away from the people on their phones as they ride their bikes or stroll a beach during a sunset…we've even heard them have conversations in public toilets! Use your ability to shift your mind instantly.

Learn to take control of your emotions by adjusting your mind to a positive thought. It may take some practice but once you start down this path you will feel better equipped to cope with stress. Sometimes when I become agitated I hear my spouse saying, "Mind Shift" as a way to remind me to take control of my own thoughts. I sometimes huff and puff and reply, "Mind your own shift," but for the most part this small technique has helped our outlook as well as our relationship.

Have you ever found yourself engaging in what started out to be a positive endeavor that turned into tears and frustration? Or something wonderful and purposeful, an act of kindness that shattered into hurt feelings and silence?

Perhaps you and your siblings decided to get together to help your parents. Inevitably, some of you will have different opinions about how this should be achieved. How can you shift your mind to avoid squabbling about procedure and keep the goal in focus? Another example is joining together to help our children in sports, music, clubs, etc. Others will have their opinions about how to achieve the objective. Can you allow them to have an opinion that you do not share? Can you shift your mind to give your assistance to fulfill the initial intention… to aid your children?

I once joined an organization to help my daughter's marching band. Each month we would meet in the school practice room to plan ways to assist our students. It seemed like a worthwhile idea, but whenever I attended I was struck by the fact that the happy musical space would turn into a hostile environment. Parents would make snide remarks, while others complained about the administration…angry voices rising to a crescendo. How was this helping? Why was I allowing myself to be involved in such unfocussed negativity? Eventually I had to leave this mob and find other more positive ways to assist the band. I wish I could have used the Mind Shift tool back then. Perhaps others could have been persuaded to see how it was a hotbed of hostility and NOT useful in any way. Together we could have shifted to a place of harmony (reflecting the music our children were playing).

By keeping this mechanism of your mind active you will find numerous ways to use it to your advantage. Some people count to ten… but not me. Nope, that's too long. I think MIND SHIFT and I have instant awareness and less wrinkles.

Even if we are the only one smiling, happy, calm person in the storm, we can make a difference. We can learn to move our anger, which is absorbed into everyone and everything we encounter, and redirect it to find ways to create positive energy and harmony in our universe. We are all connected—use Sæ-sii meditation to tune in and take control over seemingly uncontrollable events and step confidently toward a brighter future.

Practice using Mind Shift at home, and watch it spread to the world around you. This concept is a powerful tool to help bring emotional stability. Thoughts are living things—and your positive attitude may be the one element that calms a raging storm.

Lesson 8:

Embrace Awareness—
Your Parents Aren't You

Mind/Body Preparation: *It's now time for a few cleansing breaths. Breathe in slowly through your nose and out through your mouth. As you breathe in fill your diaphragm so that you can feel your stomach getting bigger and then slowly release this breath. Calmly ignore all thoughts that try to intercede and sweep clean all the stress with your beautiful slow breathing. When you are ready, close your eyes and allow this thought to fill you: "They are no longer in control."*

• • • • •

Meditation can bring healing to repressed self-loathing brought about by the thoughts of others.

Before we begin this lesson let me state that for the purpose of making this as clear as possible, when I use the word "parent," I am referring to whomever it was that raised you.

It is a well-known fact that people who have (or had, if their parents are deceased) a poor relationship with their parents carry emotional baggage that inhibits their ability to relate to others. It sabotages relationships in so many ways. You tell yourself that was then and this is now…thirty years later you are still telling yourself this. Meanwhile you have had unresolved hurt that interweaves itself into your relationships with your mate, your children, your siblings, your friends, and even your neighbors. How can this possibly have anything to do with your parents? This is something Sæ-sii meditation can help bring to the surface and resolve.

As a child when you opened your eyes each morning you found yourself in the world of someone else's ideal of what was right for you.

Yes, they cooked, cleaned, and cared for you but they also tried their best to guide your thoughts in the process. Everyone's experience is unique. You may have grown up in a home where there was screaming and violence, perhaps there was absolute silence, maybe you were raised with laughter and affection, or maybe you never got a kiss goodnight. Some of you may have been shuffled and herded like cattle in a large family, or perhaps you were one of a few, while some of you were only children. Maybe there was illness, death, and tragedy in your younger years. All of these contributed to the way you faced your world back then. But you are no longer a child and your parents' ideas of what was right for you may no longer apply or may not be correct. Perhaps it never was.

Year by year you continue to grow and your mind takes on new thoughts as you collect experience and gain new perspectives. For some, these new insights can differ drastically from opinions held by our parents and we may feel immediate tension and anxiety because it's not what we're used to. This drama plays out over and over again and even if your parents are many miles away, or even deceased, you can find yourself trying to live your life according to their ideals. This is a control that parents are able to yield over you, but only if you allow it.

It took me years to recognize that some of the things my parents taught me were basically…and I'm putting this politely…rubbish. Religious indoctrination that was rooted to their ideals was spoon fed to me. My mother's unnatural fear of anyone who wasn't Caucasian was wrapped around me like a protective shawl. Their refusal to allow us to explore new ways and new ideas because they were afraid of what the neighbors might think was oppressive. My father's favorite response to any question of his own behavior was, "Do as I say, not as I do." Yes, there were many cracks in all of this indoctrination and I chose to ignore the inconsistencies, but I tried to gain their approval regardless. Trying to get that approval sometimes meant ignoring my inner voice and stifling my own happiness. This regurgitated unexpectedly from time to time as I tried to maneuver my way through countless broken relationships. My role models were flawed and those flaws were prominent in the way I was dealing with or interacting with men who continued to disappoint me. Maybe had I been more true to myself and allowed myself to stand up against the untruths of my past I would not have tried to fix or make my mates into someone who would never exist…a father without flaws.

I don't mean that we should lay the blame for all of our problems on our parents. Of course not. Perhaps it is time to accept that their issues belong to them, and yours belong to you—period. And what about us as parents? Sometimes we pass along our beliefs not realizing they may not sit well with our children. Meditation can help us see this cycle more clearly. Once it is identified it is important to learn how to proceed. Will we repeat this pattern or remove it from our lives?

Here are a few examples from my own past that will help to better describe this awareness that awaits everyone.

I was born an artist and won several awards beginning at age seven. Throughout my developing years I had one constant desire and that was to attend art school. When I reached the age of sixteen many of my classmates were beginning the process of applying for colleges. I was excited and brought home the financial papers for my parents, along with the art school information given to me by our school guidance office. My father looked at the papers and said, "No, Lorraine. You can't go to art school because you'll never make it. Besides, you're a girl and you'll just end up getting married and pregnant." I was crushed. His words "you'll never make it" sank deep within me. Regardless of what I had achieved throughout my childhood, his criticism is what I took for my truth. Fifteen years would pass before I entered art school, quickly climbing to the top of my class. Within months of graduating I would go on to design graphics for a professional sports team and winning even more accolades. Had I listened to my father I would never have achieved this.

My teen-age son was a gifted artist who excelled in math. He was also a builder and loved making things in his school's wood shop. He was one of the top students in his graduating class and I was very excited, as I thought he would make a fantastic architect. Obviously this meant he would be heading off to college. It was a dream come true for me, my first-born flying from the nest and getting an education that would help him soar higher than I ever did. It was a windy, overcast day when this dream I held so long in my heart shattered. My son felt it was time to set me straight. He invited me to take a walk on the beach. I was happy, as I loved our time without the distraction of his siblings. I chattered on excitedly about the graduation plans and inquired which schools he was considering. He just stopped walking and turned to face me. He paused a few moments and then spoke, "I want to make this perfectly clear, Mom. I know you have wanted this for me for a long time, but I will not be going to college. I have decided to become a carpenter. It's what I've wanted to do all my life." What... not going to college, and not going to pursue the career of an architect? Was he kidding? I began arguing with him, pleading my case about the trials and tribulations of working in harsh weather. I reminded him of his natural artistic ability and his exceptional grades that would open doors to any college or university. I will never forget his reply as it stopped me in my tracks. "Those are your dreams, Mom, not mine. I have never wanted to be anything but a carpenter. I love working outdoors and I would hate being cooped up in an office. I am not asking you, I am telling you—this is my life and this is how I am going to live it." I was shaking; I felt completely deflated and I stopped holding back the tears. I admired him for speaking his truth and the only words I could mumble at the time came in a gasp, "Then you better be the BEST damn carpenter this world has ever seen!" He grew to become a wonderful craftsman and his leadership is known throughout his area. This was a tough lesson for me. I was passing on MY belief that I needed to go to college to become something better than I was. How incredible that this eighteen-year-old boy could stand up for what he believed in.

The first step in finding this awareness is accepting that your parents are just ordinary people with flaws. The iconic image that you had as a young child is just that—an image in your mind. See them as individuals who have gone through their own trials and tribulations. They have endured tragedy, joy, financial gains and losses, and perhaps some parental relationships of their own that contributed to their hang-ups and issues that played out during your childhood. You are an adult now…guess what…so are they. Stop thinking about all of those yester-years and move forward and see them for who they are, people who laugh and cry and bleed and hurt just like you. Will this realization bring sunshine and roses into your life? Perhaps not, but maybe it will bring healing, maybe it will reveal a truth that you have known all along. You are allowing your childhood impression of them to play out in your own relationships. Accept that truth and begin to move forward paying attention to how much baggage you have just unloaded. You are a good person who can begin to love yourself in a whole new way.

It was Father's Day and I was about to turn thirty-three. I was in a store shopping and kept picking up cards that said stupid things like, "Remember the time you pushed me on a swing" or, "You picked me up whenever I fell down and you bandaged my knee." My father never did any of these things. I grew angrier and wanted a card that said, "Where the hell were you when I needed you?" or, "You never kissed me goodnight or said you loved me…Happy Father's Day A#SH@!e." It was the last straw. I stopped what I was doing, got into my car, and drove with a determination that I have never known. The twenty minutes went by like a blink. I marched up the stairs to my parents' house and pushed through the front door. I startled my father as he was sitting in the same place he was everyday at 3:30PM…in front of the TV watching Bullwinkle. He took one look at me and knew I was not making a social call. He clicked off the TV and stood there looking helplessly at me. "What's wrong?" he asked. And so I told him.

"Dad, I have been so hurt and angry with you for years. I have tried my hardest to earn your love, hoping one day you would tell me you loved me. All my life I wanted to be an artist and you told me I would never make it and I believed you. I bake a stupid cherry pie at every holiday because it's your favorite, hoping it will gain me some points, I don't even know what mom's favorite pie is! As a little girl I begged you for a kiss goodnight and you told me it was too hot…and that was in January! I tried to kill myself thinking you didn't love me and I didn't because I have my own two little kids that love me beyond measure and I love them more than anything in this world. I have stayed away and never told you these things to your face fearing I would discover you didn't love me. But since I have never heard you tell me you love me I figured I had nothing else to lose. Do you love me or not?"

He slumped into his rocking chair, crumpled and visibly shaken. He hung his head and when he looked up he was crying. "I always knew some day one of you kids would come and hold me accountable. I just never knew which one."

He then proceeded to tell me that he was drunk most of my childhood years and that those days were a blur in his life. He was a two six-pack-a-day father and had only become sober three years after I moved away. He told me that he never received affection from his own mother and she too never told him he was loved and that his dad abandoned his family when he was five. He reached out and hugged me tightly for the first time and kissed me and told me he loved me dearly and he wouldn't let go of this tender embrace. We stood there in the kitchen sobbing together. Within a week both of my parents entered into therapy with me. It was only a few sessions, but those hours were filled with healing tears and laughter. My parents validated my pain and apologized for the hurt I had felt and I recognized that my father's alcoholism had brought him years of shame that he still carried.

My father contacted my siblings and told each one how much he loved them and asked if they wanted to talk about their childhood. A few of my sisters called me and said, "What the hell did you do with our father? Who is this guy?" My father was sixty-eight when I interrupted his cartoons and his life. We both blossomed and his relationships with my siblings and his grandchildren outshine any memory of the man I grew up with. We became the best of friends and I was determined to discover the man he was and not just the father who sat at the head of the table. He passed away at the age of eighty-four and I can honestly say I carry his laughter with me everyday. I was able to have more compassion for my mother, recognizing the burden of living with an alcoholic spouse. I was able to talk to my mother adult to adult, and this released so much anger that had been simmering just below the surface.

This meeting could have gone another way. He could have told me to get the hell out of his house. He could have thrown up a wall of denial. This is my own story and I share it because I know that something changed within me when I stopped looking at them as parents and started to enjoy them as people.

As you continue to meditate and quiet your mind, begin to seek your own awareness. If you feel you need to approach your parents (not all do) then realize that it can bring you a step closer to being honest with yourself and your loved ones—especially your spouse. If you cannot go to them and you want to pour your heart out in a letter, then do it that way. If your parents are no longer alive and you want to write them a letter and sit quietly as you send it up into the flames of a candle…then do it. Recognize that you can stop allowing the ideals of your childhood or the dreams that were squashed, to fall as tears on your pillow. And as you make this connection, examine YOUR behavior and see if you have been taking this out on your loved ones. Your anger, much like mine, may have been directed toward others…for years. As you become more loving towards yourself it will naturally have its effect on others.

There are no guarantees in life. Your story and your approach will be unique, as it should be. But you can start today to accept the truth that you are no longer a child. And speaking of children, by embracing this awareness you are creating a healthy environment for them as they develop, learn, and begin to make choices of what they allow into their own hearts. But that's another lesson.

Lesson 9:

Moving Thought Into Action—
How to Make Your Dreams Come True

Mind/Body Preparation: *Wow! Here we are in Lesson 9 and you are becoming more familiar with this term "thoughts are living things." Now we will see how they become a dynamic force that can bring you complete joy. Let us begin with a few cleansing breaths. Prepare your heart for a journey of peace. Feel the energy all around you as you sink into your comfy space. Relax every part of your physical state to enable your spirit to enter into this haven of tranquility. Before closing your eyes think on this: "I can."*

• • • • •

Meditation can help you achieve all the things you have always wanted to do by motivating a purposeful ACTION toward fulfilling your dreams.

As we have learned in previous lessons, thoughts are living things. When we give energy to a thought it reaches out to our surroundings and must land somewhere. Have you ever noticed moments when a thought of inspiration pops in and your whole body feels as if a light switch is being flicked on? You feel excited and happy as you give energy to this living thing called thought. Your mind begins its journey on how to bring this inspiring thought to completion. Possibilities surround this and you are bubbling with enthusiasm for this creativity and now you want to bring fulfillment to this thought, Bravo! The next part is extremely important and the key element in moving this thought into action.

When you find yourself in this state of attunement with your spirit (and that is exactly what this is), you will need to ignore any negative thoughts that might try to derail you—thoughts such as, "No one will understand why I am pursuing this." It is not about others. Or, "I can't possibly do this, it's so far fetched." Yes you can! By ignoring all negative thoughts you open yourself up to more positive ones. It is a remarkable sight to behold when, with your spirit guides willing you on, you start to move in this direction and the doors begin to open. It's as if you step one foot forward and suddenly opportunities you never thought possible come forth and allow you to create what you have been inspired to do.

The list for these possibilities is endless. Perhaps it is something of design within your home or garden. Perhaps it is with travel or even learning to play a sport or a musical instrument. Maybe it's volunteering or writing about your life journey. All of these things are there for you. Learn to accept the fact that a thought is a living thing. What you do with this living entity is up to you. You can also decide to not act and that is perfectly fine and is your decision.

Here is a simple example of moving a thought into action:

I live near the ocean and each week I take one day to disconnect from all electronic devices and head to the beach. I call this my "unplugged" day. I may read, write, paint, and always do a meditation (preferably in the water). I also like to take walks, which are usually only thirty minutes since the beach is not that long. Each time I would see trash—broken glass, plastic, and styrofoam—washed up along the shoreline. I used to step over it, shaking my head as I watched the seabirds pick among the seaweed and coral that dotted the shore. And then one day I realized if I went to the hardware store and bought a trash tool and carried garbage bags, I could do my small part in this battle against pollution. So now when I collect my beach chair and sunscreen I also grab my handy-dandy-trash-picker-upper. It's a simple effort—I was going for a walk anyway and now it has even more purpose.

Think of some ways in which you can move thoughts into action.

You mindlessly rattle off ideas all the time and tell yourself "one of these days I'm going to…" and here you sit and so many of your wonderful bursts of inspiration remain unfulfilled. It is most likely because you allowed the negative thoughts to override the positive ones. The more you practice meditating, the more control you will have. You will easily be able to decipher which thoughts are green lights and which are unnecessary thought detours and roadblocks. By listening and tuning into your positive thoughts you will become a DOER and not a talker. Learn to tap into the wondrous creature that you are and begin to follow your heart's desire.

I recently read an article about a man who has loved horses all his life. He never could afford to own one. He is now retired and has some time on his hands. He enrolled as a volunteer at an equestrian adoption facility. He has learned to give these animals tender care and in return he feels their love and appreciation for the first time in his life. His only regret is that he wishes he had made this connection forty years earlier. He learned a valuable lesson—it's never too late to follow your heart. Nothing is ever lost, only gained.

Careers, relationships, educational pursuits, or learning how to create something with your hands can all benefit from your ability to move thoughts into action. If you can think it, you can DO it.

Many years ago I lived in a suburban neighborhood where every picket-fenced-yard seemed to house a dog. I had just moved into my home and wanted a pet. I specifically wanted a collie. I grew up watching the Lassie TV show and told myself that when I reached adulthood I was getting my own Lassie. So, naturally It had to be a purebred (I no longer feel this way about purebreds, after all, I'm a mixed breed aren't I? My ancestral heritage is German, English, French…) All of the dogs I found were very expensive…yikes, $500! I could never afford a collie puppy. But for some reason my mind would not let this notion go. My thoughts, as we now know are living things, kept repeating over and over again… "There is a way to be with collies.

Keep looking." And so I tore one of those ads selling puppies out of the newspaper, hopped in my car, and drove about sixty miles from my home to a place I had never been. The road was long and winding and after a while I saw a wooden sign with a collie painted on it. My heart was beating so fast and I almost kept driving, knowing I was unable to purchase a puppy. My thoughts would not let me miss this opportunity, "GO…just have a look!" I drove down the long dirt road to the farmhouse and knocked on the door. A friendly woman greeted me and I explained that I had come to see the puppies. She gladly placed a few on my lap and I was in love. Now came the tough part—leaving without a puppy. She was a dog breeder and traveled to dog shows. This was her business, how she earned a living. I confessed that I was unable to afford them and really just wanted the chance to see all of these beautiful creatures. She sat beside me and looked into my eyes. "I am looking for good homes. I need someone who will love and care for a puppy. If you sign a paper that says you will not breed the collie or sell any puppies, I will GIVE one to you." I almost fainted with joy. She and I became very good friends and I went on to have loads and loads of collies and puppies, as I too became a dog show handler…but that's another story.

So when you have those fantastic moments when you have an incredible desire to do something and a tiny voice says, "Really? Can you actually see yourself doing that?" Smile and answer with a resounding, "YES, I CAN!"

Lesson 10:

Release the Chatter and Listen Within—
How to Communicate with Yourself

Mind/Body Preparation: *After reading this first paragraph, close your eyes and breathe deeply. Rest comfortably and relax all thought, allowing it to move away. If an impression comes to you—ignore it and blow it away with your exhale. Now think on this: "I control the volume."*

• • • • •

Meditation helps us find our silence. It is in the silence that we can discover the hidden treasure that ultimately leads us to our bliss.

We are living in a time of amplified noise. Everywhere we go we are bombarded with input—smartphones, tablets, laptops, video games, blaring radios…endless chatter all growing louder and louder. It is seeping into society every place we go.

I once visited the Louvre Museum in France. The galleries contain some of the most exquisite artworks of the great masters. I was eagerly anticipating this day and had planned it for months. I was hoping to just go and get lost in the art. After all, this was Paris, it was my first time visiting, and I wanted to soak it all in. I was quite surprised, however, to see people speaking on cell phones as they stood glancing over their shoulder at the Renoir behind them. The Louvre is home to the "Mona Lisa" and I was baffled as I watched people shoving and jostling to cue up next to this small painting and then hold their phones up to take a "selfie" of themselves with Da Vinci's masterpiece. They turned their back to the art, held up their cameras and clicked. They then moved away to look at themselves on their LCD screen, never turning around to see the actual painting. We stood there amazed as they rushed away, skipping all of the art before them, to snap another selfie standing beside "Venus de Milo." They had come to look at themselves—they were the art. There were many people of all ages doing this. Not really looking, but glancing, and racing ahead. For what purpose? To say, "I was at the Louvre. See, here is my photo." I wonder if they could even recall what was in the gallery if they were questioned. It was as if they were there physically, but their minds were absent among all of the splendor as they raced off to the next conquest of another photo of themselves.

How many times have you asked a question of someone and they replied as if they never heard the question? How many times have you written to someone and they answer as if they have never read your letter (or email)? Now think of your own responses—and be honest and critical—does this reflect your own behavior? I am sometimes guilty of this and need to learn to be a better listener. I can blame it on growing up in the hectic northeastern part of the U. S. where everyone is always in a hurry, as well as having to share the air with seven siblings, but nonetheless, I need to keep it in check. Are we so distracted with all of the static noise that we don't even acknowledge a question? How can we hear our inner voice if we won't take the time to listen to others?

As we become swamped by the noise around us, its effect can sometimes dull our awareness. We have to listen carefully so we don't miss those moments in life that can bring inspiration and lift our spirits.

I used to share my living space with someone who had been raised with a noisy television turned on non-stop. He didn't watch the TV all the time, but the white noise, the hum it created had become a way of life for this individual. If I switched it off he snapped to attention, looking about—wait—something's not right! I need my hum! I decided to detox from television; it took me a while, but I'm extremely happy I took that step. Not only has it freed up my mind, but it also allows me to stop and listen to silence. It's like finding yourself standing in a field after a snowstorm. All is still, all is beautiful, and slowly you become aware of the birds foraging for food. Removing noise and chatter and stilling the noise takes some effort but the benefits are immeasurable.

Begin to examine your responses to the people with whom you engage. If you get a letter or any form of communication, do you respond? Many people don't. And if you do respond, do you carefully read the original correspondence and reply accordingly? When someone is speaking to you, do you make eye contact, do you sit still and wait for them to finish what they have to say? Are you listening or are you racing ahead thinking of a million other things on your to-do list or drifting your attention to the chitchat around you? For me, my weakness is that I jump in and step on another's comments before they have even finished their sentence. I know why I do it—I am afraid I will forget what I wanted to say. It doesn't matter; it's still a nasty habit that I am struggling to break. I think I probably need to keep a notebook tied around my neck!

I sometimes find I am unable to focus on a dinner conversation in a restaurant because the volume of yammering in the room is invading my airspace (not even counting the people on cell phones). I am frowning about the rudeness of others and my poor dinner partner is being ignored by me...now who is being rude?

We have become a selfish people focusing on our needs and less concerned about others with whom we share the planet. If you're too busy chasing after the next thing that will bring temporary gratification, such as movies, books, video games, or what item to buy, then your conversations will be filled with "I saw, I read, I played, and I bought." Yes, it's great to have something to share with others and there are wonderful books, shows, etc., to talk about, but there has to come a time when we are not searching or doing anything. We need to practice the art of doing nothing and sitting in total silence, where the stillness raises awareness and unlocks a part of us. The questions can lead to a self-discovery that has been hidden underneath the clamor of your life. The question may be, "Am I happy with me?" If the response is yes, then soak up that feeling and settle into it, realizing that many people answer no and they could use your encouragement to give them a lift. If you're not happy, then maybe it's time to stop all the chasing that has gotten you nowhere thus far, and look within. Stop being so busy running in circles and making unfulfilled promises to yourself and others. Learn to imagine yourself in a peaceful haven that has the key to unlock all life's mysteries. Meditate on the stillness, find your field of fresh snow, and allow the muffled silence to clear away the noise so you can hear your own voice. You will most likely find yourself questioning everything in your world, re-examining some life decisions that you haven't bothered to hold up into the light. Perhaps your current path was chosen twenty years ago and you are sticking with it because this was the road that seemed appropriate then. This relates to all areas in you life—such as relational, career choices, time management, and your financial decisions. Situations change, bridges are built, and avenues to be explored are waiting for you to lift up your head and step forward.

This all might sound as if I am contradicting myself. I spoke of being selfish and also spoke of looking deep within and then following what's best for you. There is a difference and it centers on a healthy ego. Ego can overtake and puff you up as you crow loudly, thinking the world revolves around you, but a healthy ego comes by tuning into your inner voice and allowing it to sing above the commotion.

Meditation can bring you to a place where all is soundless, all is hushed. You may even find yourself being lulled by the sound of your heartbeat. Follow along this natural rhythm and don't allow thoughts to come into this private space. Drift into your silence and appreciate that you were given the wisest counsel on earth…your inner voice. Begin to clear away the commotion today and find the stillness waiting to guide you. Slow down and listen. Your loved ones can learn from your example and your senses will become more attuned to your environment. Stop rambling, start listening, and begin sharing the endless possibilities that are calling to you.

Lesson 11:

Push Your Reset Button—
It's Okay to Change Your Mind

Mind/Body Preparation: *It is time to stretch and reach for the stars. Roll your shoulder muscles and unclench your jaw. Feel your body relaxing into your space. Be aware of the silence and embrace it. Now think on this: "I have a reset button."*

• • • • •

Meditation helps us give a second look to our thoughts and decisions.

Each of us is on a journey. How did it begin and where is it going? It began long ago when you were first born. Your path throughout your early years may have been filled with love, sorrow, joy, doubt, pain, and adventure. You can fill in your own personal description, remembering how it all began. We've continued to grow in our environment, absorbing the lessons learned and collecting tidbits of information we've tucked away.

As young adults we were faced with choices. Perhaps it was to seek education, begin a career, or choose a partner with whom to share our journey. We made those choices based upon what seemed right for us at that moment in our lives. As you look at your life today, give yourself permission to ask—are the decisions I made yesterday helping me live in harmony today? This could even be a choice you made recently. Look at it closely and weigh it in your mind. If it leaves you with any feelings of doubt or unease, then it may be time to hit the reset button.

Have you ever watched a couple that lives in a toxic relationship? Years go by and they are miserably going through the motions. Why? Because of a choice they made early on that is obviously no longer working. If they truly looked within they would see that the road they intended to walk together has arrived at a fork and they are free to go ahead divided. Others may disagree with this option and by passing judgment prevent the couple from exiting the unhealthy relationship and stepping toward personal happiness. We are only responsible for the actions of ourselves. You alone know what's best for you. I personally found myself remaining in a loveless relationship believing it was the best course for my children. Not a good reason because I learned later that they felt my pain and learned to endure this, only creating more unhappiness under the same roof.

Employment is often a place we find out of necessity. Did you intend to be the cashier at the local deli? If we begin to look within we can see how our winding life path has twisted and turned, bringing us to various destinations. Some of your job opportunities may have been fantastic and others pretty glum, but each has helped you discover something about yourself if you take the time to really look within. I have had so many jobs throughout my life that it must have seemed as if I was a scatterbrain. But in actual truth, I have gleaned a little bit from each of those positions and it has helped me to be a better communicator. This enables me to be a better listener to the world around me. Money is not the only reward when seeking job opportunities.

So many of us are merely following daily routine. We get up, eat, go to our job, come home, sit in a stupor watching media, and go to bed, only to rise to the next repeated cycle. Do we continue along because that's the way we have always gone before? Does this leave you feeling good about your life or defeated? The advertising world makes billions marketing to people seeking to find a cure for this type of depression. Are you following a path that is truly your own or is it really based upon making others happy? Learn to sit quietly and allow your heart to feel the silence seep into all of the hidden corners. What steps can you take to shift into a more positive direction? We often tiptoe down the pathway of the "my life would be better only ifs." That's like dishing out ice cream and never eating it. You need to follow through on all of your "only ifs." If you have no intention of ever doing anything except yearning, then you will find yourself on a gerbil wheel chasing after empty dreams. Begin to really examine your life and see it from YOUR perspective, not from someone else's. Who are you and what makes you tick? Every person is unique and therefore we are wired differently. What are your interests? What really gets your juices going? Are you attracted to certain subject matters? Have you ever asked yourself why? Do you allow yourself to get lost in something you are passionate about? It's only when we are honest with ourselves that we can begin to recognize the hopes and dreams that have been stagnant too long. Now is the time to air them. Today is the day to open your mind and breathe in the possibilities of your heart's content. If your life needs some readjusting…hit that reset button and start fresh. Set your intention to move in the direction that will create a happier you.

If you are in a toxic relationship, have the courage to revisit your initial decision. I am not advocating a break-up or a divorce. I am simply saying hit the reset button and be honest with what you are CHOOSING to continue, because this is truly what you are doing. Don't get bogged down in the "only ifs." Meditate, find your island of peace, and understand that you may have to make a new path for yourself. It will benefit your loved ones, your partner, and especially you. If I hadn't quit a high paying graphic design job to swap it for a meager paycheck in a pub I probably wouldn't be writing this. By I did hit that button, even though financially it made NO SENSE to anyone including my children, and I drove over 1300 miles to find my paradise. It is DO-ABLE. I say this with experience. Allow yourself to THINK AGAIN.

As you continue to use meditation to uncover the precious treasures that await you, life will seem to taste a bit sweeter. Your voice may become a touch softer and your smile seemingly wider. By hitting the reset button you are giving yourself permission to move your thoughts towards a better tomorrow. Yesterday is no longer important and your "only ifs" are a reality waiting for you.

Lesson 12:

Vibrational Check-Ups—
Tuning Into Your Heart's Song

Mind/Body Preparation: *Breathe in the positive environment all around you and exhale all stress. Relax into the silence of your own breath. Before closing your eyes, allow a thought to settle into the comfy chair of your mind: "I am energy."*

• • • • •

Meditation helps us tune into the Earth's good vibration.

Humans, plants, animals, and the world around us are all made up of energy. In fact, they are living energies. Your energy is much like your fingerprints; nothing existing can match your personal vibrational signature. Imagine your energy as a light radiating all around you. Now imagine each element you come into contact with as a living, breathing ball of light—your loved ones, friends, pets, each glowing. Now close your eyes and imagine a person you love with all your heart coming into the room and standing beside you. Can you sense the shift in your energy? Take note of the changes within you. Do you feel lighter, more vibrant, calmer, or even tingly? Keeping your eyes closed, imagine a person who is always irritable and unkind, someone who always has something nasty to say. They come into the room and stand beside you. How has your energy shifted in response to this person? Note the changes within you and how your energy reacts to this negative energy standing beside you. We can begin to see how one individual, whether positive or negative, can change the dynamics in a room like a rippling wave washing over it. This is the effect you yourself have on other people. Now you can begin to have a deeper realization of the "good vibes" or "bad vibes" you are connecting with. You are able to become more sensitive to this as you tune into it. This unspoken communication resides all around and perhaps you may be engaged in it totally unaware. So, what kind of energy are you?

Now that we have identified the feelings of energies, let us move toward tuning into them. Think of your energy like a device that runs on fuel. Begin to make the connection that your energy is reliant on the choices you are making every day. What types of foods do you eat? What liquids do you consume? This beautiful bundle of energy requires certain foods to make it run smoothly. Begin today to make wise choices when you approach each meal and strive to give your body the very best. You certainly do not need another diet book to determine what is best for you. Listen to your body and give it the nourishment it requires to run more efficiently. Just like a vehicle that needs certain products to keep it humming, your body runs best when you select nutritional nourishment. Science teaches us that up to 60% of our bodies are composed of water, the brain 70%, and the lungs around 90%. The carbohydrates and proteins that our bodies use as food are metabolized and transported by water in the bloodstream. Replenishing this water is extremely important. So now think about your own patterns. How much water do you drink daily? We have become a society that has replaced water with beverages loaded with additives. Your body will run on this but less efficiently and perhaps some of your parts will become unhealthy and break down. Water is the tool that transports waste material from your body. Sugary beverages only add to the toxins. How much water do you need to drink? Learn to tune into your own energy and give it what it needs. Make intelligent choices.

For years I was unaware of the effects that negative energy brought to my health. I was living in a toxic relationship, not bothering to make any changes. I wore it as my punishment for my out-of-wedlock pregnancy. At the time I was allowing religious dogma to rule important life decisions. As you can imagine my home life was a hotbed of negativity. I suffered from insomnia for many years. I struggled with depression, as well as a poor self-image, loathing my appearance and myself. My miserable life was all hidden behind a smile as I cut the slices of anniversary cake that marked another year of despair. Pretty extreme example, I know, but once I made the connection that living with all that negative energy created a toxic swamp making me unhealthy, I was able to pull myself out of the muck and swim to fresh water. Is it any wonder that I eventually chose a place named Clearwater to call home?

As you continue to learn more about yourself through meditation, you will see that certain activities enhance your energy. Food and water are not the only things your energy requires. Look within. What makes your heart sing?

All my life I have lived near water. I have always been drawn to the sea. As I began to learn more about myself I found that my many walks on the beach fed my creativity. This is my element, this is my energy booster, and making this connection was like finding a magic that I could tap into. And so in order to maintain a healthy me I have set time aside each week to disappear from electronics and the blathering of the world to be near the ocean. I use this whenever I need to recharge my batteries. How do I know when it is time to do this? Easy—if I skip this practice, within days I am feeling restless and irritable and I know I have to take a break.

How are you recharging your energy? What is it that helps you feel rejuvenated? Perhaps it's creating something or being in the presence of animals. Meditate on this. Maybe you love mountains, hiking in a forest or sitting beside a babbling brook. My spouse loves to build and create things. He loves taking many pieces and bringing them all together and for him this creates an inner calm. My sister has always been drawn to horses and she finds that they create a peace within her that is unexplainable.

Learn to surround yourself with the elements that bring you harmony. Look around your home, workplace, and your community. Does it reflect this balance? Does it remind you of the things that make your energy feel healthy? Recognize the necessary components that keep your energy burning brightly and embrace them. Maybe you're someone who loves gardening, or listening to music. Perhaps you enjoy browsing antique shops or learning a new craft. If you are unable to do these things as often as you would like, perhaps you can decorate your home or office space with photos or reminders of what it is that resonates with you and YOU alone. For me, some of my most inspirational moments have come while sitting in water. I am drawn to images and sounds of water. What about you—where is your energy booster? Once you discover what it is that really makes your heart sing, be sure to include it in your routine, knowing that you are forging a path to a healthier you. This is your energy maintenance and only you will know what works best for you. As you learn to connect with this you will be contributing to the good vibes needed on our planet.

Lesson 13:

Rising Above the Negative Input—
Tune it Out and Protect Your Energy

Mind/Body Preparation: *When you are finished reading this first paragraph, close your eyes and take three deep, cleansing breaths. Breathe in the stillness all around you and exhale all tension. Relax into silence. Now allow a thought to settle in: "I am LISTENING to me."*

• • • • •

Meditation helps us hear harmonious communication and move away from empty chatter.

Learning to listen to your inner voice can be very helpful when trying to comprehend what others are saying. As we begin to connect with our higher self, less and less noise filters in. The noise is what consists of empty chatter. I often refer to this as the "he said-she said" talk. It's when someone tells you their reasons for doing or not doing something and it all revolves around someone other than themselves. How can you move away from this endless finger-pointing and make positive pathways to harmonious communication? By learning to listen to your own voice FIRST. By tuning into your higher consciousness, you will be better equipped to identify when this empty chatter arrives on your doorstep.

If you feel you are misunderstood, then ask yourself, "Do I understand myself? Have I identified what it is that is truly bothering me?" Often it isn't about what you thought it was. Instead, the reasons others may not understand you has to do with YOU. How? Because you are too busy reflecting the cause of your unhappiness onto others. It must be THEM, it can't possibly be me.

Here's an example of how you can apply this in your everyday situation.

Two people are discussing how terrible it is that a couple they both know are going through a divorce. One person supports the wife, the other defends the husband. The discussion becomes a bit heated and uncomfortable. The voices become clipped and the energy in the room is crackling. What just happened? The two people are discussing a choice about divorce made by others. They may not like it, they may have opinions regarding it, but they have not taken into account that it is an action brought on by someone or both parties that are married choosing to end the relationship. Time spent dialoging the "he said-she said"s will not change the outcome. Perhaps the people in the heated discussion are looking at their own relationships, their own spouses, their own difficulties. Maybe they are in a toxic relationship or perhaps they were raised by two people that should have divorced. The point of their distress over the break up of the couple they are discussing may not be about the divorce, it may be about their own inability to connect with what is so troubling. Meditation can bring this to the surface. Meditation can allow your mind to move to a positive place instead of remaining locked on past events.

Here is another example. A college student phones a parent and is crying. The student lives on campus and is going through various trials. The parent immediately wants to have this conversation in person but it isn't possible because of the distance. The child continues to share all of the woes of life—relationships, exams, homesickness, and lack of sleep from the noisy, sloppy, roommate. The child is experiencing the pangs and pains of moving away from home. The parent is swept into the drama of the moment. Naturally they want to fix it and begin to tell the child all of the ways to make it better. The child blusters at the parent's notion to interfere and the communication becomes stalled. Now the child wants to disconnect and the parent feels that their child is hanging from the edge of a cliff and really needs help. The call ends and the parent is left with tension, worry, and doubt. The student hangs up and calls friends to let them know that things are better now and plans are back on to go to the party.

What just happened? The child just downloaded on the parent. The parent felt helpless during this emotional conversation and somehow felt their duty was being challenged. The reality, however, is that the child was learning to deal with the transition into adulthood. It's often a bumpy road, and had the parent taken the time to step aside from the tears they would have probably heard their inner voice saying, "Many others have gone through this natural transition." The stories may vary with the events and details but basically it is a sign that the child is stepping away from the nest and learning how to fly on its own. Meditation can allow this to be seen for what it is. Meditation can help us sift through the drama and teach us how to protect ourselves when others download their negative energy onto us. It's natural, of course, for a child to reach out, but the parent can also learn to see that the child is just testing its wings. They can remain calm and apart from the stress as if looking from above. Listening, not fixing, is what the child wants. Meditation teaches us all to be better listeners.

There are many ways to apply this to your normal everyday routine. As you learn to sit in silence and quiet your mind your ability to NOT think can help you during times when you least expect it. As you begin to recognize that thoughts are living things you will be more guarded of what you allow into your mind. Media will no longer be an automatic source for your information, as you will acknowledge YOU are in control of what your mind allows in. When you are waiting in a line and others are discussing things that you know to be untrue you will not be drawn into the negative chatter, but will shut them out and tune in to a more pleasant thought. As you are sitting in the bleachers watching your child in a sporting event the ugly comments about the opposing team will not be acknowledged and you will be able to enjoy the time spent encouraging your child. When you are helping a senior citizen and they are repeating a story you have heard a dozen times before, you will be able to smile as you can tune into the moment realizing they miss their careers, their busy days, and just want to relive it by telling you their history. You don't have to listen to the story, but you can listen to their heart.

Meditation can help you realize that you have a filter and it is waiting for you to access it. Once you begin living your life by choosing which thoughts are allowed in and which are not welcome, you will see that your load will seem lighter. YOU will feel lighter. This ability to listen to your inner voice can bring about a change in you that will reveal a love of self. Thoughts that were placed upon you by others will no longer matter. Opinions of you held by others will simply be seen for what they are—opinions that do NOT belong to you. You will be able to see how truly beautiful you are and you will want to take better care of yourself. This ability to love yourself will change your life and you will wake up and see that you have had this all along and you are finally acknowledging it. Once you have found this you will be able to connect with a bliss that no dictionary can describe. This is what meditation can do for you.

Lesson 14:

Lessons Our Children Teach Us—
Wise Counsel Comes from All Ages

We have arrived at Lesson 14 and by now you may be wondering if I will be giving you tips and tricks to meditation. For those who like to skim a book and jump ahead, I will save you the time. There are NO FAST TRACK ROUTES TO UNDERSTANDING YOU. By choosing this fifteen-minute daily practice you are in the "development" phase of your journey. If you do find yourself sitting in the dark, looking at a blank screen in silence, then consider yourself advancing along at a pace that is perfectly NORMAL. A blank space is the perfect place for your higher consciousness to send you inspiration. This inspiration does NOT always happen during the actual fifteen minutes you are sitting. So let us continue with the understanding that you are a work in progress.

Mind/Body Preparation: *Settle down into your chair and take three deep, cleansing breaths. Breathe in the tranquility around you and exhale all stress. Relax into silence and allow a thought to settle in: "I know the TRUTH." Close your eyes and pause a few moments.*

· · · · ·

Meditation helps us break the cycle of unhealthy repeated patterns that could otherwise lead to dysfunctional families.

As we move through our busy lives we carry thoughts that have been embedded within us for many years. Like lint left in the dryer they can build up and if not examined and removed can become combustible. Some of these thoughts were placed upon you with the greatest affection and with a loving intent, but they were not actually for your best interest. They were actually thoughts that belonged to a loving adult who thought they were being helpful.

Here are some examples of how left unattended these thoughts can become quite harmful to the way you think of yourself.

When I was a young child my parents told me that Santa's elves were always watching and if I was not on my best behavior then I would not get any toys for Christmas. How did I respond to this? I became fearful of windows. I was afraid to use the toilet, worrying about pointy-eared pixies peeking at me through the window. Thankfully my big sister stood watch and I didn't wet myself.

As I moved into my pre-teens I was warned against holding hands with boys. My mother told me holding hands could cause me to become pregnant. You can imagine the laughter as I tried to warn other girls on the playground about the evils of holding hands.

As an adult I was reprimanded by friends who, thinking they were being helpful, warned me about the "well known truth" that God hates divorce and that I should prepare for his wrath should I leave my toxic relationship.

I carried so many of these un-truths for a good part of my life and I wore the negative energy of fear like a cloak. It was through meditation that I recognized the origin of those thoughts, and finally accepted the truth—they were NOT my own.

Now let us examine some of the un-truths we place upon others. Here are some examples of mine.

At the young age of nine my son asked to take trumpet lessons. "No way!" I said, "I am not paying for lessons that you will end up quitting. Trust me I know about these things."

What I didn't tell him was that when I was nine, I had tried clarinet lessons and squawked so badly I ended up quitting. Years later his sister would ask me for music lessons and I consented; she went on to become a very talented musician and writes and composes her own music. Later my son reminded me of how much he had wanted to learn the trumpet and asked why I had held him back. I felt horrible because the truth was that I was the quitter and I had made him feel it was something he could never do. He never did learn to play an instrument, but he has two little girls and I wonder how he will respond if they ask to take music lessons.

I told my daughter at age eight that no college would accept any student who ever got a C in school. I was enrolled as an adult in Art School at the time, and earning straight A's. She was tearfully trying to match my grades, and coming up short; she was filled with self-loathing. It was years later that she brought this to my attention. Rather than focusing on grades, I should have told her to simply do her best. Why? Probably because my parents wouldn't allow me to go to college and I was determined that my daughter would enroll.

My youngest son was born following his two over-achieving siblings. He was a poor student and always dragged his feet with homework. I had been a parent of honor students, not F students. I became frustrated and after all else failed I told him, "Your brother and sister never had poor grades, why can't you be more like them?" I cringe even writing this as it really sunk into his heart and he carried it with such deep pain. He believed he was worth less and that he would never gain my approval. Why? Because I too had been a poor student and hated those red lettered F's I brought home to have signed by my angry parents. He has gifts and talents in many areas and I finally was able to correct myself and allow him to feel his true worth. I was able to see the damage MY thoughts had caused and luckily was able to acknowledge them and together we released them. This is a powerful step towards achieving self-love.

Can you look at your own life and see that the truths your parents may have instilled in you may be far from the mark? Can you see that they were just ordinary people probably passing along some advice because of their own baggage they had been carrying from something that was placed on them? As you can see by the examples above this is something we live with every day. Upon careful examination we can begin to unravel the thoughts placed upon us by others and acknowledge that they are not our own.

Maybe you have been carrying something from your past. Perhaps a feeling of unhappiness lingers over past relationships, a parental disappointment, or just a nagging sense of feeling less than others. As you sit in meditation allow your higher self to recognize the origin of those painful thoughts you have been wearing and release them. It is time for them to GO. Find your truth. We carry the thoughts of our parents and grow into adults who turn around and place them on our children and loved ones. Recognizing the truth will help you break the cycle. Take a deep breath and release all feelings of LESS and take better care of the thoughts you put upon others. Begin to use your quiet meditation to heal yourself and in doing so you will begin healing others.

Lesson 15:

Societally-Conscious Guilt Trips—
Your Opinion is the Only One That Matters

Mind/Body Preparation: *As we begin this lesson let us shift our focus for a moment. Hold up a hand and look at it. Study each finger, visually memorizing the grace of each part. Now slowly turn it palm up. Look at your fingerprints. They are yours alone. Now sink down into your comfortable chair and relax. Take a few cleansing breaths. Breathe in slowly through your nose and out through your mouth. As you breathe in, fill your diaphragm so that you can feel your stomach getting bigger, and then slowly release this breath. Calmly reject all thoughts that try to intercede and if they do venture in, just IGNORE them. Before closing your eyes think on this: "My Thoughts of ME are BEAUTIFUL."*

· · · · ·

Meditation helps you see your inner beauty.

People continue to capitalize on the poor self-images of others to earn a living. Wow…let's examine this more closely. Magazines touting edited glamour photos appear everywhere. Their message? If you want to be truly beautiful you must look like a super model. Millions of dollars are spent in advertisements aimed at making all of us feel we are somehow lacking in our appearance. Obviously, the manufacturers of these products continue to benefit or their messages wouldn't be plastered on the sides of buses, appear as banners on our favorite websites, or interrupt the music we enjoy on the radio. It's a mountainous amount of media aimed at selling us products that are supposed to make us feel happier. Whether we are just standing in line at the grocery store or driving in our car, these messages have crept into the corners of our minds and interrupted our intimacy, affecting how we feel about ourselves.

Now is the time to use all that you are learning in Sæ-sii meditation to tune into what you allow to seep into your thought process. Quiet your mind and close your eyes. Think of some of the areas where society has created a standard that you feel you must meet in order to "appear" in good standing. Here are some examples:

- Home
- Car
- Education
- Products or material purchases

Do you feel this makes you more valuable? Do you use material possessions to measure your worth? Before you answer too quickly, pause and think it over.

For many years, I wore makeup. As my salary increased the cost of it grew higher as well. No longer was I buying brand X. Oh, no, it had to be a big name because its perceived value meant I was finally better than brand X. This all came to a halt the day I was sitting in a restaurant and a woman in her fifties, trying to look her twenties, walked past. The fact that she was wearing too much makeup triggered an "aha" moment for me as I saw it for what it was—a costume. I am not saying that wearing beauty products is wrong. Not at all. Many people take great pleasure in this and it is a personal choice. I began to understand that I was continuing to wear makeup because I had been seen with it in public for so long that without it my identity would somehow be… less. Was this true? Was the opinion of what the world saw in me truly how I valued myself? NO. And so now I wear it when I feel in the mood, and very little if that.

How about our choice of cars? What makes us buy the brands and models that we do? I used to feel horrible driving a used car as I noticed every dent. Seeing shiny new cars parked alongside mine made me cringe as I slid behind the wheel. Was I willing to make those huge car payments to dress myself in a new vehicle? Well, actually, yes. Like many others I signed on the dotted line and harnessed myself to years of debt to drive to a job that was only five minutes from my home! What was I thinking and what did I actually gain? My income at the time was probably just enough to cover that car payment. New cars are great but too many people continue to search for the latest model when the one in their driveway is suiting them perfectly well. Now I have chosen a home where I can walk or ride my bike to most destinations. Lesson learned, money saved.

Now let's talk about our clothing. This applies to both sexes, as I have known a few men to have enormous wardrobes. When I was a small child I shared a few dresser drawers with my sisters. We lived in an old house with tiny closets, and since we had eight children and only three bedrooms, we shared every inch. Now think of how many clothes you can fit in a standard chest, triple dresser, and small closet. Divide this by four and you can imagine the space I was allotted. I am not complaining; I am just stating the facts. As an adult I branched out and it felt marvelous to have some space to fill, but did I need all of it? For years I loaded furniture and closets with all of my clothes and rotated my seasonal apparel from their hiding place in the attic. That was then. Now I have only a small walk-in closet (no dressers) that I share with my spouse. It contains built in drawers and few feet of space for hanging items. This space holds everything we own including seasonal wear. My new rule is this—if I purchase a blouse I have to donate a blouse. Why? Because I have learned that I am happier living with less. I use every piece of clothing I own because I have less to choose from. If something wears out I reward myself with a replacement. Look around at your own clothes and how you approach this management. Perhaps like me you were caught up in the way society views our wardrobe. More apparel does not always improve self-image. For some it actually brings them down as they stare at the items they wish they could still fit into. Don't even get me started on the dieting industry; let's just say many of them are gazillionaires feeding off of our inability to understand our true qualities.

How we see ourselves and how others view us can be totally different. I recently came across a video created by a forensic artist focusing on this issue. The artist sat at a drawing table never looking at a person seated behind a screen. The subject was asked to describe him or herself, and the artist drew their portrait. Next the artist had a third party go behind the screen, study the subject's facial features and describe that person for the artist, who made a new portrait of the subject. The artist repeated this with several clients. He then showed the subjects the two drawings he made of them. In each case, the drawing created from the subject's own description of him or herself was far less attractive than the ones created from the description from a third party.

This points out that we need to reevaluate how we perceive ourselves. We are each more beautiful then we think.

Look within and see your beauty and the rest will work itself out. How? By using meditation to strip away the societal guilt placed upon us from years of trying to be something other than who we are. Connect with your true spirit, embrace your beauty and try not to bury it beneath a mask.

Lesson 16:

Your Journey is Not a Competition—
There is No Enlightenment Certificate

Mind/Body Preparation: *Slowly begin a few circle breaths, breathing in through the nose and out through the mouth. On each exhale feel yourself sinking deeper into your chair. Relax all stress as you feel your beautiful rhythm beating with the heartbeat of the universe. Just before you close your eyes, think on this: "My journey is not a competition."*

• • • • •

Meditation helps you find the path that is designed to fit you alone. It helps you to stop chasing after the approval of others and focus on your road to bliss.

From time to time I meet people who want to know if there is a faster route. How can they achieve "better results" in meditation? I politely listen as they recall all of the stories they have read and heard about the mystical journeys of others. If this is what you are looking for, I suggest you stick to the fantasy section of your local library. I am not saying that you won't ever find yourself experiencing the unexplainable, but if this is what you are seeking, then you may be setting yourself up for disappointment. As you progress, always keep in mind that you are moving along at the pace that is absolutely perfect for YOU.

I understand the desire to go-where-no-one-has-gone-before. It's natural to want to experience the kinds of things we see on the big screen. Who wouldn't? Some people have dreams about flying or becoming different animals. How marvelous for them. Smile and listen and enjoy those moments as they share them and realize that this is part of THEIR journey. Yours is yours alone and if it isn't exotic don't feel that you haven't attained anything. Bask in the understanding that you are being carried along on a river of peace that is taking you closer to an amazing discovery of self-love.

If you become discontent with your "dull, not-so-exciting meditation journals," remind yourself that you are a work in progress. You are filled with imagination and wonder and each time you sit in silence you are strengthening the connection to your uppermost YOU-ness.

Can you remember when you were a student and the kid next to you seemed to be able to do math with his eyes shut? Or that student who excelled in art when you were lucky to draw a stick figure? Then you all ran outdoors to recess and perhaps that same kid who could create wondrous works of art couldn't even catch a ball. Does it make one better than the other? No, of course not. Each of us is created differently and each of us will have meditation experiences aligned to our spirit.

One of the things that I can tell you with certainty is this—wanting to have a mystical experience doesn't make it happen. Even if you set your intent and really want it badly, the wanting isn't the vehicle to achieving this. Allow yourself to just accept your journey exactly as it is intended for YOU.

I once attended a workshop and listened to the people around me exchanging stories of their magical encounters during their meditations. Some said, "Try my way, it really works," while others would counter, "But you just need to go to more workshops if you really want to have enlightening experiences." Enlightenment...really? Who is the keeper of this enlightenment certificate? Who determines what is enlightenment and what is not? As I sat wide-eyed I wondered what made their journeys seem so much better than mine? What was I searching for? Maybe it was time to re-think this meditation I was doing. And of course that was when I was "doing" meditation as an act and not sitting in silence. That was when I was "waiting" for something to happen instead of allowing the natural connection with my higher self to appear in its own time. I'm thankful for this encounter with others because I saw that it was being discussed almost as entertainment. Entertainment was NOT what I was searching for. No. I was searching for an inner peace. Ask yourself the same question. What are you searching for?

Use Sæ-sii meditation to develop your ability to "let go" and remove yourself from this unspoken community of competition. I am quite sure if you challenged some people they would deny it and say, "Oh, no, I don't really see it that way!" Really? Then why are there so many websites and products selling courses on developing states of higher consciousness? Why are people seeking and searching and collecting certificates? What is the true purpose? When does the collecting and searching stop? When do people sit in silence and just BE?

When we can sit in silence and become comfortable with who we are, we are moving toward a place that can help others. Look around you. There is heartache, sadness, self-loathing, and people feeling they are just barely surviving. By finding your own inner peace you can begin to shine a way for others. This is what I hope to achieve. This is how I will measure my progress. Learn to accept that your journey is your journey, not a competition, and be happy with who you are.

Lesson 17:

Keeper of the Treasure—
Your Experiences are Priceless

Mind/Body Preparation: *As we approach this next lesson imagine yourself holding a shell to your ear. You cup it against your ear and all falls silent. The stillness within this shell has a message for you. Imagine the ocean from whence it came, lapping along the shore. Breathe with this rhythm slowly in and slowly out. Each time the waves roll back allow yourself to sink more deeply into your chair. Before you close your eyes allow these waves of thought to wash over and envelope you: "MY thoughts are VALUABLE."*

• • • • •

Meditation brings abundant treasure. This treasure leads to a happiness that is beyond words.

As you practice daily Sæ-sii meditation it may begin to take on various forms. It may bring you astounding insight, brilliant messages elaborately designed in colors and hues never before seen, flashing lights that are so bright you wince. They may come with a song, a beautiful melody playing over and over again. You are floating along and slowly you realize there are words in the tune waiting for you to unravel their message. You may get total darkness and a stillness of serene peace. Whatever you experience the first thing to remember is YOU are the receiver and YOU are the only one that can interpret it. Many people will offer to help and give you possible translations for the "symbols" given. Are they symbols? That is for you to find out. Keep writing in your journal and watch the synergies begin to take shape.

For example, if you are given an image of an airplane, is your airplane referring to an airplane or does it mean something more? If you were to ask ten people, each would give you a different meaning. They might say, "It's about transportation, no it is about transition, wait it's about moving your attention to a higher place," and on and on. It isn't for them to know. It is for YOU. Keeping a journal will help you to see the language your higher self is speaking. Some people get total blackout during meditation and later on will instantly recall something revealed to them. They will write a long detailed account and be astonished at what they discover. It may come in bits and pieces over days, weeks, or months—little shards of light shining upon your journey as you meditate daily. What does all of it mean? This is for you to learn and discover. It is YOUR connection to your higher self to your spirit to God, Source, Is, Creator, or whatever you choose to call it. No matter what your belief, this is for YOU.

One of the best ways to find answers after journaling meditations and dreams is to talk about it. It is your spirit giving a voice to thought. Naturally you are excited as you begin to experience moments in your journey that seem monumental. Even though you are inclined to tell everyone who will listen, learn to pause and give yourself time to just let the words appear in your journal and sink in. Digest this experience and let it speak to you in the language meant only for you. If you are fortunate enough to have a loved one who will listen, then go ahead and share away. But keep in mind that you need to choose wisely what you are about to say because your meditations are your treasure box of YOU. When you're in the early stages of meditation try to hold back the urge to shout it from the rooftops. If not, you may find yourself being laughed at and ridiculed. You don't want your personal journey to become the blunt end of a joke as family members snicker around the table. Where would your island of peace be then? This is not what your treasure was intended for. Take the time to hold your precious experiences and collect them into your safekeeping until you are ready to understand them better. I am not saying that you will miraculously be able to understand all symbols or clues, but you will be able to see that you have a unique way of hearing your inner voice. Remember, it is speaking to YOU. Sharing can be a wonderful thing as you find yourself wide-eyed, reliving the messages coming forward, but realize that to others it may seem like you have...how can I put this politely...lost your mind! They may get quiet and nod and then call a family meeting to have your head examined. Well, they probably won't go that far, but they will not be able to help you decipher anything and might leave you feeling as if you are "less" than what you are. You are not less than anything; in fact, you are a beautiful spirit living in a physical human body. Perhaps that is the greatest element of meditation—the wondering.

Here are some examples from my journal that I have kept to myself...until now...

January 5: I meditated early this morning. I see myself in my kitchen watering houseplants. THE PLANTS STARTED TALKING TO ME. One had a deep male voice and he was describing the chemical elements in the water. I asked if I was doing everything all right and did they need anything? It said I was doing wonderfully. I then asked another question, silence. Then I felt stupid talking to plants and tested it again by saying, "bye," as I watched myself turn to go I heard him say, "Bye." Man, would I love to be a plant whisperer!

November 8: I see sparkling water and then I see a bird silhouetted in flight begin to rise and fly higher and higher. I know instantly it is my daughter. I watch as she flies high against the orange and red sky at dusk. I say to my guides, "Is this my daughter as a bird?" I am told, "She is not earthbound and this is her time to soar." I see another bird off in the distance flying but not able to reach the same heights—I know that she is unlike this lower flying bird and is gliding easily overhead as the other bird flaps and tries to reach height—and then it vanishes.

As you can tell by these two passages, they sound surreal. Who would believe that I was communicating with plants? How did I instantly know that this flying bird was my daughter? These are my visions, my treasures.

Meditation is not only wondrous, it also causes you to stop and question. You begin to examine all thoughts. Are they yours or someone else's? Do they originate with you or someone presenting a truth? Is it truth? Who wrote your history books, the winners or the losers? Yes, this is one of the most extraordinary aspects of meditation. By learning to listen to your inner voice you begin to rely more on your intuition. That intuition is often unexplainable to others, but you KNOW what you are feeling and sensing, and you know it is correct for YOU.

Whether you decide to tell others or hold on to these gems of intuitive awakenings is your choice. Allowing them to settle and seep into your life will determine how you approach each day. In time you will find what works best for you. There are many social networks with people sharing their meditation experiences if you want to pursue that avenue. Find what works for you and always remember that you hold the key to the treasure box.

Lesson 18:

Toxic Relationship Residue—
How to Remove the "Dis Ease"

Mind/Body Preparation: *As we continue to meditate, our other senses may become enhanced. You may begin to smell scents you never realized were there before. You may hear sounds more acutely. Taste may become enhanced and the touch of an embrace may seem more loving. What is happening? You are becoming more connected with your higher consciousness. Take three deep, cleansing breaths using your circle breathing. Sink deeper into your chair on each exhale. Relax and blow away all stress. Follow along on this day-dreamy state into a place of peace. Before you close your eyes allow this thought to wash over you: "I can love myself."*

• • • • •

Meditation can detox unhealthy thoughts that have been deeply rooted. This may bring about a change in your physical body as you release all negative energy.

By examining the living thoughts we have collected through the years, we can see the torn and tattered remnants of negative relationships still lingering in the shadows. Whether they are spousal, community, or workplace relationships, does not matter. If they were harmful, they have left their mark. There are people who will come and go throughout our lives, much like chapters in a book. It is important to validate each of them and accept them for who they are and what they meant to you. Some of the characters in your life story may have been unsavory.

I have a few of those characters in my life that I would rather forget. Revisiting these negative experiences holds the energy and brings it to life. By opening up these living thoughts we are actively awakening negative energy. This unfavorable energy attracts more of the same. It can bring damaging effects such as insomnia, headaches, irritability, mood-swings, and lack of concentration, just to mention a few.

When you look at your life today, examine the current chapter and see if you are keeping the residue of past toxic relationships alive. If you have moved on from a disturbing lifetime experience yet still feel yourself hurting, then it is time to LET IT GO! How can you do this? By using your ability to switch off all memories regarding harmful thought remnants that are holding you back. You are actually being held captive by your own mind. Take responsibility for what thoughts are allowed in and guard your beautiful space. You may try to convince yourself by saying, "Oh, but that was years ago. I'm way past all of that." This is all well and good. Your subconscious, however, still brings it forward every now and again, causing you to feel "less" about yourself. You are actually fanning the flames of negativity every time you revisit it.

I have lived with violence, experiencing both physical and verbal abuse. These negative occurrences left me filled with insecurity and hatred for the weakness that I thought represented who I was. It took me years to extract myself from this. Meditation helped me to release the energy that kept this self-loathing very raw. I would pick at the wounds of my heart like a scab, keeping it bleeding. This did nothing to help overcome the pain and did everything to bring me poor health. Years ago I had the privilege of working as a volunteer with battered women. I sadly watched the abused victims return to their destructive environments again and again. Many seemed like tethered boats tied securely to the dock, unable to sail freely toward open peaceful waters. It was their thoughts that held them there. Thoughts like: "I have no money, my children need both parents living together, it's not as bad as I think it is." One of these victims said this looking at me through two black eyes, while holding a small infant that had suffered a broken arm in an angry burst of violence. She was in denial of the danger she was living in and she was allowing her child to remain in this horrific lifestyle.

Toxic relationships will continue to bring you disharmony until you recognize them for what they are. They are serving you absolutely no good.

As you proceed with your meditation, see these thoughts as negative energy being released in each exhale. Blow them away. Let them leave your peaceful, beautiful self and allow them to exit now and forever. Poof. Gone.

This applies to ALL relationships in your life. Employment, neighbors, relatives, church, school, clubs, organizations, and spousal relationships can each harbor unhealthy energies. If you have lived through a phase of disharmony regarding thoughts, words, or deeds, you need to release this energy. See it for what it is and move your thoughts to a more positive environment. Positive attracts positive. Move in this direction by only accepting thoughts for your highest good. Remember you are in control of which thoughts are allowed in. Negative thoughts bring "dis-ease."

When you release this through meditation, any negative thoughts that have been lurking in the shadows will be brought to your attention. You can now validate them and LET THEM GO. If you are engaged in an unhealthy relationship, it will become clear to you that the path you are treading will require a conscious choice. Do you want to continue with this or is it time to move toward inner peace? Only you know what is best for you.

Allowing your inner voice to help you rise above the negative input will help you make better decisions. Meditation enables you to tune out all thoughts and quiets your emotions—reinforcing self-control. Your choices are made calmly and with integrity. Will meditation solve all toxic relationships? Of course not, but it can help lead you down the path of self-love.

Loving yourself attunes your attention to your true value and self-worth. You are a beautiful person who has a right to live in peace. Meditation helps you to discover all the wonderful things about YOU. Your eyes will be open to new opportunities and exciting possibilities. Your heart begins to realize it can love and BE love to the world that so desperately needs this positive healing energy. This love begins with thought. Meditation brings thoughts of self-love that can help you proceed along your journey and navigate away from the residue of toxic relationships.

Lesson 19:

The Good Odd—
Popular Opinion Doesn't Instill Harmony and Self-Love

Mind/Body Preparation: *Take a few moments to relax in silence. Roll your shoulders and stretch out all kinks. Lower your head and do a few neck rolls. It feels good to just let all tension go. Now feel your feet rooted to the ground and allow this balance of the earth to connect with you. Breathe in and out evenly and when you are ready to close your eyes, take this thought with you: "Being different does not make me wrong."*

• • • • •

Meditation enables you to give yourself permission to NOT follow the crowd.

As I continue to teach the art of Sæ-sii meditation, I am often struck by the fact that to some this appears—odd. Hmm, it does? I do? To most people I am a bit weird. Okay, I'll own that. If I seem odd to you, that's perfectly fine with me. I must confess, I am a happy odd being.

Coming from a background where everyone actually believed everything written in newspapers, TV, and on the Internet, it took me a while to extract myself from media. I began my journey of switching off in 2005. I no longer read newspapers, watch television, or get my news from any media that I haven't triple checked. I refer to this as my detoxing from TV phase, since this is where it all began. It has allowed me to better tune into my inner voice. The more people with whom I shared this concept the more they thought I was absurd. How can switching off the PAID programming that is being drilled into our heads seem insane and when will people start thinking for themselves? I am not saying that everyone believes everything they read and hear, but how do you know that an idea or belief is truly resonating with YOU? Removing yourself from the thoughts and opinions of others, including the media, is not the path we are taught to follow. If you meditate and listen to your inner voice, you may learn that most of the stories being touted as national news are speculative hogwash couched in, "This may happen or this could happen," or some hyped-up version of a worst-case scenario. What I am teaching is an easy method to hearing YOUR INNER VOICE, a voice that belongs to YOU. Am I saying you have to throw away your TV or computer to find your bliss? No, but you may want to reexamine how much time you spend allowing others to bring you their opinions and ideas. Are you being manipulated?

Have you ever seen a situation comedy without the laugh track? The audience NEEDS to be told when to laugh. Well, if it's funny, you laugh; if it's not, you don't. This seems the most logical path to me, but it is now so embedded into the audience that if the laugh track were removed it would seem…odd. Are you simply being manipulated into following the crowd? Choose for yourself what is humorous and what is not. Remove the laugh track and listen to what your inner voice is telling you. It's okay to be the only one not laughing.

Look around and begin to see the differences in people you come into contact with. It can be work, family, your neighborhood, or a spiritual organization, it doesn't matter. There are many people who are very much NOT like you. You may even wince, thinking how strange they live their lives. This is how I used to view the community I lived in. That's until I realized how others viewed me. People may be odd and different, but this does not make them wrong.

When I was around eight years old there was a young boy on the playground who was always absorbed in looking for bugs. The children teased him and called him names. He had Multiple Sclerosis and was pale skinned and very fragile. He could not run and play or 'fit in" with the group. He had very few friends and it wasn't until much later that

I learned he was ill. We always just thought he was a bug-nerd. He had collected albums and albums of specimens. I would see him walking home alone carrying some insects in a jar. Later, in junior high school, he was the top student in the science class. He was very special and yet he seemed quite odd.

When I first started down this path of inner exploration I lost a few friends along the way. I am not trying to frighten you; I am merely stating a fact that some will not be able to stay in your circle. You will be gravitating to a place where you are very careful to whom you listen and who you allow to spread negativity within your space. Remember, negative attracts negative and positive attracts positive. Friends who you thought cared for your happiness, may actually smile but think, "I am not getting the response I wanted. I am no longer able to vent or download my problems. I can't talk about any TV shows or gossip because she (he) has switched it all off. This is no longer serving me so I'll go call another person and ask them over for lunch." That is okay, this is a necessary clearing of your energy field and it is a revelation that this "friend" was using you. Lesson learned. Let's move on.

Imagine yourself seated among strangers in a crowd. All of your energy is swirling and mingling as you are gathered together. A speaker turns on a microphone and begins to tell you something. His words are spoken eloquently but something feels off. You disagree with parts and you sense that what he is saying does not resonate with you. What do you do? Since this is a hypothetical example, we will imagine any response is possible. This is Lesson 19 and by now we have learned how thoughts can come and take root within us. Keeping this in mind, how do you proceed? Well, if you are like most, you will sit quietly and applaud when he is finished, smile politely and then drive home disgusted. I did this for many years and I have finally come to realize that I was GIVING AWAY MY ENERGY to the being standing before me spouting out all of his opinions and views. I suggest another option. Approach EVERY situation you encounter where others are voicing THEIR opinion and recognize that it belongs TO THEM. You do NOT have to give your energy to their thoughts. If you are able to, I propose you exit as quickly as possible. If you cannot exit then take all of the tools you have learned thus far and let your mind go to a place where you can SWITCH OFF and rest. Call it daydreaming or zoning out, but give yourself a mental break. Are you being rude? No, you are being the GOOD ODD. You are protecting yourself from taking on something that does not gel with you and your higher conscious is actually protecting your energy.

Here is another excerpt from my meditation journal:

September 5: Meditation: I saw sparkling water and it became moving, flowing, tiny pieces of tile all forming a mosaic pattern of different shapes and patterns. They were like this wave of tiles washing from top right diagonally to bottom left and they would change patterns in a fluid motion. They were just stunning and I was waiting to see if they would become something other than random patterns—and then it ended.

Odd? Yes. This journal entry looked quite strange, but a year later I would cover a space in my home with the pictures I saw in the meditation. I designed a mosaic mural in my bathroom that took me over one hundred and thirty hours to complete.

September 9: I ask to speak with my parents and I began thanking them for the dream I had the previous night. I tell my mom how wonderful it was to see her with her hair up in curlers, as it felt so intimate. The feeling of her as she led me down the hall filled me with intense love. As I was thanking my parents I am aware that I am seeing their living room and a large tree-sized flower arrangement being delivered. A hand appears and takes a white card attached and brings it closer into my view. It is addressed to me, "With love from Mom and Dad."

Strange? Perhaps, but I am certain with all of my heart that my parents use my connection time to send me love. Dream visits may occur more often once you use meditation to connect to your beautiful spirit. My heart is not doubtful because I, and many others, have had visits and conversations in their dreams with loved ones.

As you continue on your journey of self-realization, you may appear peculiar to many around you. Tread with confidence and hold your head up high. This is a sure sign that your inner happiness is radiating.

Lesson 20:

Smiling Through Broken Glass—
Your Life Experiences Are a Work of Beauty

Mind/Body Preparation: *As we come to this part of the book I hope that by now you see how unique you are. Your meditation process is moving along at a pace designed specifically for you. It is a daily routine that is short yet magnificent. At first it really does seem ridiculous as you sit in your room with your door shut, alone in a dimly lit or darkened space. Your family members may shrug and say, "Whatever floats your boat." Wonderful. This is exactly where you are the healthiest—floating along on your pathway to bliss.*

Let's continue as you begin your circle breathing and allow your body to relax. Slow your breathing and sink deeper into your space. Drift into this stillness of your breath and before you close your eyes, think on this: "I am many parts."

• • • • •

Meditation shows you the wisdom and inner strength gleaned from the ups and downs of life's experiences.

I used to think that my life was nothing more than shattered dreams. I was never able to quite win the approval of my parents. My teachers shook their heads disapprovingly as they marked my grades in red ink. And I always wished I were born into a family that was a little less lean in the wallet. Being born into a crowd, you learned quickly to take whatever was offered and to be thankful.

As I mentioned earlier, I learned at a young age that I had a talent to create art. My silly drawings won me awards beginning at the age of seven. As I became an adult I was happy to discover I could actually earn a living by doing something that came so natural. I had no formal training but it didn't stop me from trying. I even made it all the way to New York City, where a big company wanted to purchase some of my art for their children's clothing. Wow, and I was just a nobody illustrating children's wear out of my garage. And then something happened that would change my life forever. My art representative stole my portfolio containing all of my original work and sold my designs, passing them off as her own!

It was like a meteor crashed into my world. I had been moving in a direction that seemed so perfect when, BAM, I was knocked flat on my back. I had a few options available to me. Take her to court and submerge myself in legal bills and a swamp of negativity, wallow in self pity and numb myself with drugs and alcohol and sink deeper into depression, or go to art school and learn how to develop the natural talent I had arrived with on the planet.

First I would have to get my hands dirty and put in the work. Did I mention I was a single mom during this time raising an eight and thirteen year old?...Um, yeah. I drove one hundred and eighty miles daily, five days a week for two years to earn a degree so I could say I was an "official" artist. I was determined to do my very best. I can still remember telling my classmates who thought I was an over-achiever. "I didn't drive all this way to get a C!" What I discovered after graduation was that no one ever asked to see my certificate. All they wanted to see was what I could do.

The theft of my portfolio helped move me toward being the artist I am today. Do I want to thank this woman? No, I wouldn't exactly go that far, but I am thankful I was able to rise above the negativity and move THOUGHT into ACTION.

We must all understand that life holds a lot of broken bits and pieces. We have storms and trials and we sometimes fall flat on our face. It is how we are able to create something from this that enables us to love ourselves more. It helps us feel complete, whole, and beautiful, and allows us to soar.

Now let's look at your life. What obstacles have you been faced with? If you were to draw a timeline and list the emotional highs and lows, you would see that through the years you have been molded and shaped into the person you are today. Imagine those experiences as tiny bits of broken glass. Try to stand back and see yourself as a work of art. Yes, you have collected many stories along your journey and each can be seen as a tiny piece of you. Your strength, your wisdom, your grace, and your laughter are encapsulated in every broken piece of your life. See these experiences for what they are—your mosaic of YOU. Embrace the fact that you are much more than what you see in the mirror. You are many parts, and you are beautiful.

Lesson 21:

Removing Drama From Trauma—
How to Become More Emotionally Stable

Mind/Body Preparation: *Before you read this next lesson—and if you are able—let's just stand and stretch. Arch your back and roll up into a standing position and reach high above your head. Now return to your chair and settle into your space. Feel your feet firmly on the floor and imagine them growing roots into the earth. You are connected to this beautiful energy. Begin slowing your breath and relaxing down into your chair. Disregard all sounds and move along to the rhythm of your heartbeat until you come to this thought before closing your eyes: "I am in control of my emotions."*

• • • • •

Meditation teaches you to pause and step away from emotional energy that may derail you. It is a self "time-out" that can bring a necessary calm that will help you face a crisis, should one arise.

There are times in your life when you are faced with storms. An illness, family struggles, an accident, spousal issues, loss of employment, death, financial woes…the list can go on and on. If you are not in a storm now, you can rest assured that there is probably someone you know who is going through one. How we navigate the storm is more important than the storm itself.

You're a being made up of molecules that are vibrating with energy. All around you is your energy field. What passes through this can affect you. Standing beside an angry person in the elevator can infect you. As you continue with your meditation you will begin to understand how the mechanism of your mind operates, as well as how your energy can be sapped and drained. When you are tired, you are not able to stay focused. If you are hungry, you are unable to quietly listen to a loved one's story. If you are sad, you may not be able to applaud or share in a congratulatory event. As you move forward on your journey, look at the living things called thoughts and try to see them outside of you. This ability can help you see areas in your life that are creating stress when they shouldn't even be allowed into your energy field.

I have faced many storms in my life. I don't need to list them, but believe me, I could probably fill up many pages. I have learned to recognize them more easily when they blow in unexpectedly. They will continue to knock on my door as long as I breathe. This is a fact. How can we use meditation with these blustering trials and tribulations that seem to pop up every now and again? By learning to recognize the unnecessary drama during the trauma.

I once visited Istanbul. It is a beautiful old city filled with such incredible culture. I love its people and enjoyed my visit immensely. We arranged to meet my daughter there. I especially loved the sound of saying, "Meet me in Istanbul." She was flying from northern California and met with several mishaps along the way. If you travel, you are familiar with airline services being quite unpredictable. While I sat in my comfy hotel room sipping a strong cup of Turkish coffee, she called me in a panic. After many hours of postponed flights the airline representative had informed her that they did not have a confirmed seat. Her voice depicted utter exhaustion, and she was unable to hold back the tears. She was frustrated and the battery on her phone was about to shut off. The plane she was supposed to board was ready for departure and she had not even made it through security. I told her I would try to call the airline and straighten it out. Now I was becoming upset. It was a situation over which I had little control. I was feeling her anguish and her crying voice still lingered. Luckily I was able to stay calm and tell myself that although she may not make this flight, we would still see each other, just not at the time we had first expected. My spouse is a very calm, cool guy and immediately called the airline, gave them her confirmation number, and suddenly the impossible became possible. A representative walked her to the head of security and placed her on that plane! As you can see, the story could have gone a different way. I am sure you can recount your own disastrous airport adventures. The old me, the non-meditating me, would have collapsed into a crying bundle of emotions, destroying the memory of our vacation. Having the ability to rise above the drama and keep the positive flow moving helped me start to switch my mind to PLAN B. What was Plan B? Most likely she would arrive a day later and our time together would have been just as wonderful.

Here is another example. I once knew a woman who was the leader of her neighborhood association. One of the neighbors had put up a fence without getting the proper permission. She and a few of the other association members felt angry over this. They had meeting after meeting and finally agreed to hire a lawyer. Each homeowner spent thousands of dollars in legal fees fighting over this fence that was built without the proper paperwork. Over time some neighbors stopped speaking to each other. They became hostile and stopped interacting as a community. Children who had been friends became enemies. A few marriages even broke up over the financial stress of it all. The case finally ended and the fence was removed, but every family in the neighborhood association had spent over ten thousand dollars to accomplish this. Not one person had ever bothered to walk over and speak to this neighbor when he began to build the fence. They were all so caught up in the drama they never even realized they were creating their own trauma. Can you see how negative attracts negative? What if it was you sitting in that initial meeting. Would you be able to see through the drama?

Learning to see thoughts as things that reside apart from us can help protect us from being caught up in these painful experiences.

I grew up in a home with many children all fending for attention. We played long hours outdoors and had our share of bumps, bruises, and scratched knees. I can still hear our parents, as we would run to them crying over our latest injury. They would take a quick look at our boo-boo and say, "No blood. Stop crying and go back out and play." In the years following, my own children would come to me in tears over occasional stubbed toes or minor injuries. My parents words would fall from lips, "No blood. You're fine. Go back and play." This may not have been the best approach, and I am not advocating ignoring your children, but my parents' attitude taught me to recognize the difference between minor and major. Can you see this in your own life?

One day I was enjoying a cup of tea at a friend's house. Birds were singing and the sky was blue. She was someone I loved being with, a delightful companion. The phone rang and she politely excused herself and picked it up. Suddenly she was screaming. I mean SCREAMING; howling; screeching! She dropped the phone and fell to the floor. Now she tossed and turned like someone having a seizure and continued sobbing. I ran to her side asking her what had happened. She ignored me, rolling up into a fetal position and crying hysterically. I was becoming frantic. I was alone in a house having tea with a sweet woman I thought I knew very well, yet suddenly had my hands full with a very out-of-control person. What in the world was happening? Slowly she gathered herself and sat up. "I'm sorry," she said. "I'm okay now."

"What's wrong?" I asked. "What happened?"

"It's horrible," she said. "My brother's daughter didn't score high enough on her tests and now she has to go to a community college. Can you believe it? This is so shocking for our family. I come from a family of doctors and lawyers. Oh, what will this do to my father?"

I was so stunned I could not speak and exited as quickly as possible, leaving her to call all of her relatives and recount the event. She clearly made her own storm. This brought her insomnia, weight loss, and the need to pressure her own children about their schoolwork. Seeing this first-hand made me realize this negative energy was something I did not want around me. We must set boundaries between acquaintances and friendships. Each of us has an electromagnetic zone—known as the auric field—that surrounds us; it picks up good and negative energy. Be on guard and use your ability learned while practicing daily meditation, to LET GO of negative energy. Release it. Poof!

Meditation can help you face the many ups and downs along your path. If you are struggling financially perhaps by clearing your mind you will be able to see it may only be temporary and find a light at the end of the tunnel. If it is more serious, perhaps by clearing your mind and sitting in silence you will find new pathways to make it less stressful. If you are dealing with grief, perhaps you can use this meditation time to give yourself a time-out from thinking of all that you miss. Allow your higher self to comfort you in a way the world cannot. If you are ill, use your meditation to see your beautiful spirit that is unblemished and perfect. It knows you better than anyone. Ask for healing or ask to be shown coping tools to endure whatever you are experiencing. Allow this peaceful tool to help you through the waves of emotion so you can float along a current of silence. The silence may bring you a new attitude and with this you can be better equipped when the winds gust and the rain begins to fall.

Interlude—
A Time of Reflection

Let's pause and take some time to reflect on what we have learned. In the beginning I laid out all of the steps to help you look within. If you practice daily Sæ-sii meditation and listen to your inner-voice it increases self-love and may lead you to your bliss. How are you doing? Are you following all of the steps? Have you set apart a special place and time and approached it with the attitude that this is your development time? Are you able to spend a little more time in silence each day? Are you able to see that thoughts are living things? Here are some common questions and answers that may give you some further insight.

Q: In the beginning I was very excited about all of this and could do it for a few minutes. Now, I am disappointed that nothing is happening. How can I know I am getting anywhere with this?

A: When you first started you probably could NOT THINK a thought for a few mere seconds. By now it is probably a few minutes. You are in your development stage and if you continue doing this daily you will be able to go into your space and "switch off" instantly. Be assured that the "happening" part is very gradual.

Q: Why don't you use music, candles, or aromas in meditation?

A: Good question. Many people use props to help them relax and release all tension. While you are in your home this is great. The method I teach will help you meditate when you really need to zone out quickly. For example, when an argument breaks out nearby and you can't really say, "Hold on. I have to go light my candle," or when someone in the workplace is complaining about a co-worker. Or when you're in a hair salon and they are spreading mean gossip. You can quickly tune it all out without the need to put on music, light a candle, or burn some incense.

Q: I started doing this daily and was really enjoying it, but then I felt guilty and I'm finding it hard to stick with it. How am I supposed to find my bliss if I have so much work that needs to get done?

A: Perhaps you may not be ready for this. Or maybe you are not seeing the benefit because you are allowing the guilt to override the peace. Closing a door to the world, shutting your eyes and sitting in silence is an act of HONORING YOURSELF. You need to make the connection that you are valuable. See this as a necessary act that will bring balance to your busy schedule. Try changing the time you meditate to just before you open your eyes in the morning (see answer to next question). Your mind will not be able to think of chores when you are in that in-between time of wakefulness.

Q: I have followed all of the steps and I am still frustrated because of all of the distractions. I will zone out and a dog will bark or an ambulance will bring me out of my daydream state. Why can't I do this?

A: Meditation is not about doing and you should never feel frustrated…ever. When I first started down this road I was exactly where you are. I would shut my eyes and just settle into a wonderful state of relaxation and the cat would start meowing outside of my door. My eyes would pop open and I would instantly become agitated. Then I switched my meditation time to dawn. I did not leave my bed as I slowly became aware that I was crossing over from sleep to awake and I would quickly recite my prayer and drift into a meditation. Try this for yourself. Dawn is a wonderful time because the world of distraction is not yet up and about. Just try not to fall back asleep.

Q: I have been getting some images and thoughts during meditation but by the time I go to write them in my journal I can't remember them. How can I improve my memory of what I am experiencing?

A: Many students have this same problem. Try adding a notebook and pen into your meditation routine. Always keep it close by and then begin the meditation. As soon as you finish and say your thank you to the universe, begin writing. Record any smells, sounds, images, sensations, or thoughts. Write how you feel at the time you come away from it. These notes are your road map and in time they will show you some wonderful insights. You don't have to write complete sentences when you first come out of the meditation. Jot down bullet points to capture it for memory and then sit down and write it out in your journal as soon as possible.

Q: Can I meditate in a group or do I have to do this alone?

A: Yes, you can always gather together in a group and blend your energy by sending love to one another and the universe. But it is also important to continue your private alone time meditations. Outside interference can hinder your development. Remember, the people in the group have their own lives filled with anxieties and life situations. Learn to LET GO on your own before joining in with others.

Q: You talk about "protection" in the opening invocation. Why do I need protection?

A: As we open ourselves up to the ether world or unknown regions of the spirit world, we must be aware that all beings are not positive. This request for protection creates an atmosphere of safe passage as you connect to your higher self, helpers, guides, or what some refer to as guardian angels. You only have to recall an unpleasant experience of a nightmare to snap you into the understanding that you want the highest and best for your connection at all times. This is exactly why we end with a blessing and thank you to the universe. You are dis-connecting or hanging up the phone to the ether.

Q: I am following all of the steps and have been meditating for months and I still feel I am just not able to LET GO. Am I missing something? Maybe everyone isn't wired for this silent meditation.

A: Wired may be the key word here. Look about your space very carefully. Do you have any electronic devices powered on? You cannot sit with a cell phone or computer muted; they need to be OFF. Shut down anything that has an off button. Look to see if you have any high voltage power lines near your home. It may seem silly, but you are a vibrational being that is a ball of energy. Some of these devices can actually block your connection to your higher self. If your living situation does not allow you to power off, then you may need to find a new quiet space. Whether its tucked into a closet shut away from the family or sitting under a tree, it doesn't matter. Find your haven.

Q: Can this be taught to children?

A: Absolutely. Teaching a child to honor themselves at an early age is a lifelong tool. Can you imagine how grounded we all would be if we had started this process early on? I have taught children to do this and their parents are amazed that they shut themselves into their rooms and ask not to be disturbed. The children have given themselves a fifteen-minute time-out. By sharing meditation with all that you meet, you will create more harmony in our world.

Q: I am so excited about all that I am discovering. Some of it feels magical. I don't feel comfortable sharing it with my family or friends. Who can I talk to about all of this?

A: Wonderful, I am so happy for you. In Lesson 17 we spoke of your experiences as treasure that you kept in a box. You are wise to follow your intuition and guard your experiences while you are learning to explore meditation. There are social networks and meditation forums with others just like you who talk about all that they are learning. Take time to explore some and find one that feels right.

Sample Meditation Journals From Readers

Together we can learn so much by sharing all that is given. Throughout the lessons I have presented samples of my own Sæ-sii meditation journals. Here are a few from others who use daily meditation to enrich their lives. Keep journaling and watch your own treasure box begin to open. I would love to hear about how you are using Sæ-sii meditation to follow your bliss. Write to info@calicohorses.com or visit my blog:

http://meditationapathtohealing.blogspot.com/
or https://calicohorses.com/lorraine-turners-meditation-blog/

Dorothy writes:
Meditation: I hear "you prepare, I'll provide." I see a farm with rows of flowers, organic, reusable farming, a park-like setting. Before me are actual plans drawn to create a community ecologically planned out to reduce and reuse.

Helen writes:
Meditation: I am outside in my favorite chair. The birds are chirping so loud I think to myself it is distracting and I hear a voice say, "This is your meditation music." It's a cloudy day but I feel bright light on my face and I wonder if the sun has broken through the clouds. I know instantly it's love energy. My meditation music plays on and I relax. I see a path and follow it to the edge of a pond. The trees and lawns look so perfect and I think it took a lot of work to get it so perfect looking. I hear it takes care of itself. I move away to a street with people sitting on benches talking. A small town feeling comes over me.

Marie writes:
Meditation: I am shown the yin yang symbol. Keep the light and

the dark balanced. Be the dots and walk the golden line between the two. Balance is required. A balance of light and dark. The moon could not exist without the sun and the day could not exist without the night. Balance.

Nathan writes:

Meditation: Sparkles of light. Dreams are reality taking firm birthing of mind's love's endearment. Love is all these things and more. Give, share, and, repeat. Love moves beyond mountains, beyond terrain of any kind. It is seamless—be seamless, don't cut into pieces the fabric of love. Weave the love into great works of art just as it is. Love. Give love, share love, feel love, every being.

Charles writes:

Meditation: I calmly reach out and connect to my spirit guides, and I feel a sense of belonging. I ask to be one with the universe, and send love and calmness to my family that still exists on this level. I tell the universe that I want health and abundance, sharing specifics each time. I open my eyes and feel peace.

Dawn writes:

Meditation: I was in a desert area, walked into a dark house, saw skeletal remains of a baby, but I remained calm. I had trouble leaving because I saw no opening. I heard my guide say, "Walk forward. Do not turn back." So, I did. Walked forward and an opening appeared. Now it was no longer all desert, it was desert on one side of the sand dune and ocean on the other.

Mark writes:

Meditation: Slept through meditation. Seem to slam back into my body. Don't like that feeling.

Anna writes:
Meditation: Someone is humming a song. I can recognize it.

Victoria writes:
Meditation: I was told time is not linear, that it is a spiral going up or down; allowing us to be in several dimensions at the same time; allowing us to live and experiences. Hence time travel and shape shifting.

Eliska writes:
Meditation: I imagine traveling through the colors of the rainbow. I was suspended in dark space, with stars all around. Each color was represented on a staircase that was made up of glass block, glowing with radiant color. At the top of the stairway, I saw a beautiful doorway, also glowing with wonderful colors and light. It looked so far away and out of reach. Then I heard a voice direct me to look behind. And I saw how far I'd already come.

Sandra writes:
Meditation: I have been taken to an outside theater. On the screen was ME…I was literally beating myself up then I realized the people who were watching the movie playing on the big screen were all my angels, guides, spirit helpers. I looked again at the people watching and some are upset and appear to cry. I hurry past the screen to see a long country road and my guides stationed at posts along the way… motioning me forward and encouraging me to, keep going, I have almost finished this leg of the journey. I can see my guide Tallfeather and he motions me through and says, "Onto the next leg, my child!"

Lesson 22:

Decreasing Clutter Increases Clarity—
Clearing Away Stuff Brings Coherence

Mind/Body Preparation: *Find your comfortable space and begin your circle breathing. Slowly breathe in to the count of six and pause. Now slowly exhale to the count of six. When you come to the pause feel yourself settling deeper and deeper into your seat. Do this three times. Now breathe slowly in again and on this exhale take this thought with you before closing your eyes: "I am filled with order and balance."*

• • • • •

Meditation allows us to discard that which is no longer needed.

Think back to your childhood and try to remember what your living space looked like. Were you a messy person? Were you a neat freak? Or are you some who says, "Who cares, I certainly didn't pay it that much attention."

We are going to take an imaginary trip and float like a weightless energy all about your current living space. Let us examine it closely by doing a mental sweep across your home. Pause along the way and get a really good mental picture before proceeding. Follow along every nook and cranny and examine all of your possessions. If they belong to others, disregard them for now; we are only looking at things that belong to YOU. Now move to your closets and carefully look inside. Pause here… can you look with your mind's eye and imagine this? Next, let's move to your drawers. Pull them open, lifting up everything. Are clothes folded or stuffed? Pause and see this. Then take a good look at how you have arranged things on your shelves. Can you identify the items? Do you see anything piled? Pause and look all around. Move on to your computer or laptop, if you have one, and look inside the folders. Do you need all of this information? Look at the dates. Look at the contents of your email folders. Make a note about the amount of data you are storing. Can you see all of the items that belong to you? Good.

Continue on and look around the outside of the dwelling. You are like Superman with X-ray vision and you can see though sheds, garages, and storage spaces. You have all of this stuff placed in areas all around you. Examine every inch of it carefully and slowly. Now let's float over to the vehicle that you drive, remembering to disregard items that are not yours. We are focusing on YOU. Look in the glove box, the seats, under the seats, and inside the trunk. Take a thorough look into every personal space that concerns you. Okay, now let's focus on where you work. Look at the space all around you. Again only at the areas that YOU have some influence over and come into contact with.

Allow your mind to return to your chair while we continue with this lesson. How did that make you feel? Are you wishing we never brought this up or are you comfortable knowing your things are in good order? I used to be that person who would probably skip this lesson, as I didn't need some nosy person looking into my closets and junk drawers. But this is not a lesson in neatness; this is a tool to help us better understand how we see ourselves. When our lives are out of balance, that disharmony is often reflected in the places in which we live. How are they related and what does this have to do with meditation? If you feel you are someone who has balance and order in your living space, then BRAVO, you are in the minority and you will most likely be able to LET GO of thoughts more easily.

As you continue along this path of moving your mind away from all thought during your meditation time, you will begin to see that you can also LET GO of physical objects that no longer serve a purpose.

If you live with others, you may want to raise your hand at this point and say, "It's not me, it's them!" Well, let us begin with you and your things. Bringing harmony and finding your bliss begins with you taking a good look at you. Others may benefit by your example.

I have lived in many places since moving from my parents' home. I loaded moving vans and carried my belongings wherever I ended up. Once I even moved to a place so small I had to pay for a storage unit to keep my things. This became pretty pricey to keep stuff indefinitely. Eventually I had a yard sale and dispersed of it, but only after I spent a lot more money on the rental space than I collected selling my possessions. Over the years I have moved all of my belongings like a turtle—carrying everything I had eleven times before landing where I am today.

When I decided to end my unhappy marriage and move to Florida, I knew I would be leaving most of the things I had accumulated all of my life. This is not something I am recommending to anyone. I am just stating the fact that I was aware that I was saying goodbye to material items. Did they still have a purpose? Perhaps, but I just wasn't sure where or how they would fit into my new space. I can still remember the day I packed. I had made a checklist of what I could fit into my small car. My computer equipment and summer clothes were high on the list. But the dishes, pans, linens, and furniture just didn't make the cut. When you are faced with downsizing to survive, you have to think fast. This taught me a very important lesson. Material items are not my most treasured possessions; my relationships with my loved ones are. I left him with the contents of our home and I took the peace in my heart, knowing I was moving to a place of self-love. I couldn't sit on it or cook with it, but discovered a happiness that is priceless.

As we look about your material possessions, let us try to simplify your living space by introducing a little more order into it. Do you feel that you don't know where to start? That's okay. Do you feel like you have no reason to start? That's perfectly fine too. But, if you want to begin to unravel some of the clutter that has been weighing you down, you will need to take fresh look at everything you have been keeping. Remember that thoughts are living things and by hanging onto things your thoughts may be dragging you back to a lot of "stuff." Begin by picking one area; it can be a drawer, a closet or a cabinet. Remove everything in it and clean it with a cloth, getting every piece of lint. Now look at the items that you have accumulated over the years. Begin to separate them into four piles. Keep, Toss, Donate, or Sell. Keep in mind that the more items that are kept tucked away in hidden places the less likely you are to use them. When you are finished, sit down and think about how this makes you feel. You now know exactly what is in this space. You have sorted it out and your mind is able to LET GO of the stuff that was held inside. Can you see how this organization helped clear your mind? It can actually make you feel lighter. You developed this tool of LETTING GO each time you meditated.

You can choose to do this with everything you own. You can take out the items, hold them up to the light, and ask yourself, "Are these still serving a purpose?" If not, then LET GO of them. If you follow this example and slowly organize your things, you will feel better about yourself. If you are a pack rat it may be more difficult, but here too is a lesson. Why do you hold back? What thoughts are you keeping inside? Use meditation to release all that is no longer bringing harmony and begin to recognize the order and balance it can bring.

Lesson 23:

Good Vibrations Bring Good Health—
How to Let Your Inner Light Shine

Mind/Body Preparation: *Before we continue, let's stand up and stretch. Spread your arms wide and really stretch. Stand up on your toes and reach for the sky. Release all tension and do a few shoulder rolls. Now come back to your chair and settle in. Take three deep, cleansing breaths and on your last exhale carry this thought with you before closing your eyes: "I can raise my VIBRATION."*

· · · · ·

"If you want to find the secrets of the universe, think in terms of energy, frequency, and vibration." — Nikola Tesla

Meditation raises our awareness to the kind of energy we give off every day. Our positive energy can bring about the necessary changes that will help us move our thoughts into action.

We are vibrational beings. Each of us is a ball of energy with a unique vibration. When we are in balance we are in harmony with the frequency for which our vibration was designed. A healthy being has a high vibrational frequency of around 62-72 Hz and when it drops to lower levels your body can become susceptible to colds, flus, and various forms of dis-ease. The definition of frequency is: the number of occurrences of a repeating current flow per second. Your vibration affects your mind, body, and spirit. Much like that beautiful tiny bird that flits about, you are actually humming.

Each day you wake and slowly recognize thought. As we have learned, thoughts are living things. When you allow yourself to reconnect with your conscious state you become more aware of your first thoughts. They can be about food, work, family, or household chores. Regardless, you are pulling your energy to a thought. This thought can either raise or lower your vibration. Seeking to raise your vibration helps you to increase your ability to connect to the power of intention. What is your power of intention? It is your ability to MOVE YOUR THOUGHTS INTO ACTION. We must move from spending days, months, and YEARS thinking about what we want to accomplish into actually DOING IT. Raising your vibration gives you that extra spark that can help you fulfill your greatest dreams.

If we were to incorporate a daily routine of waking with positive thoughts, it would begin our day with a boost of internal energy. After all, we are all energy and we all vibrate on different frequencies, so why not strive to be your very best?

Before I began the practice of Sæ-sii meditation I had no understanding of vibration. I was unaware of how my energy was affected by a high or low frequency. I just thought that I had good days and bad; emotional setbacks filled with tears and sporadic laughter that made its way through my gloom and doom life. I was also lowering my vibration each time I would dwell on negative past issues. Every time I had a pity party, or something harmful from my past drifted in, it created a dip in my energy. Sorrow, depression, anger, and hostility all lower your vibration. Some people turn to alcohol and drugs when they are dealing with issues and this can really send you into an energy free fall. When your vibration reaches a lower frequency it can be very difficult to bring it up again. I learned more about how my life was being affected by vibration when I began meditation. It changed my outlook and I began to pay better attention to my daily routine.

I can honestly tell you I am now a very happy person. I laugh regularly and, to the best of my ability, have removed myself from negative energy. I still am faced with trials and tribulations, but for the most part I feel my health has improved by finding ways to raise my vibration.

What about you? Do you feel you are a happy person? Perhaps you can find ways to improve your situation.

Here are some ways to help raise your vibration:
1. Become conscious of your thoughts. State positive affirmations daily. "Today is a new day and I am a beautiful person ready to accept what is for my highest good."
2. Continue to use Sæ-sii meditation daily. Connecting to your higher power and intuition will allow you to rise above the negative thoughts that can lower your vibration. It does not matter for how long. It only matters that you DO.
3. Become aware of the foods you eat. Consuming foods that are covered in pesticides will make you feel weaker. Processed foods filled with chemicals will actually lower your vibration. Seek to include organic, fruits, vegetables, soy, nut, and virgin olive oil to help raise your vibration.
4. Reduce drug and alcohol consumption. Not only does this lower your vibration but you will find yourself surrounded by low-vibrational people that enjoy this habit. Limit it or remove it from your life completely.
5. Tune into the music you are listening to. Does it have messages of love, passion, hope, and forgiveness? Or are the lyrics filled with anger, hate, and resentment. Words are powerful and can contribute to the way you feel about yourself and others. Monitor what seeps into your life, whether in the car commute to work or the background radio in your home.
6. Low-vibrational television can derail your good intentions. The constant stream of negative energy is not good for you. The mixed messages of real life dramas featuring crime, violence, and hatred interspersed with commercials telling you to buy a product to bring you health and happiness will lower your vibration.
7. Surround yourself with high-vibrational people. Family members

and friends who are always speaking with a glass-half-empty attitude can drag you down. Limit time spent with this type of person and connect with high-vibrational people who are filled with happiness and joy.
8. Look around your home to see what you have chosen to view everyday. Photographs, books, art, crystals, plants, and the colors in your home can all create energy. Learn about feng shui today!
9. Incorporate a lifestyle that includes being OUT in nature as often as you can. This will raise your vibration and put you in touch with a community that is sharing our planet. Learn to listen, smell, see, feel, and KNOW the energies that want to connect with you. We share the same natural resources and man is NOT above all life forms. Raising your vibration will make you more aware of the needs of others.
10. Wear or place crystals and minerals in your personal space. Some of these minerals vibrate at a very high frequency. By connecting with their energy, your vibration will lift to meet theirs. Some high vibrational crystals are: Kyanite, Rainbow Mayanite, Zincite, Aura Quartz, Gaspeite, Moldavite, Ajoite, and Bookite, to name a few.
11. Laughter is one of the most important elements used to raise your vibration. Let's look at it a little more closely.

I was raised in a family that seemed to have more to cry about than laugh, but I had the good fortune to have a parent who used laughter to combat negative energy. I look back in wonder, remembering the threatening letters and phone calls from bill collectors. I marvel at how my parents stretched a tiny paycheck to clothe and feed eight kids. Yes, of course there were many tears, but it isn't really the lows that have stayed with me. It is the laughter. I remember once, when my father was asked to speak at his sister's 80th birthday, he began a little story that started out, "We were so poor they invented welfare to feed us.

Our house was in such disrepair we had to paint it to condemn it. As kids, we stole the bones from our neighbor's dog to make soup, and when the dog died we thought we killed it." On and on, he continued, and the entire crowd was laughing so hard they were in tears. Yes, these are the tears I think of when I recall those struggling days of my youth.

What about you, how often do you laugh? Surround yourself with people who bring joy to your life. We do not always have the ability to rise above our daily woes and sometimes we have to deal with grief, illness, and despair. Yes, there are very real situations that some of us must navigate along our journey. It is in the realization that we are on a journey that allows us to see possibilities of something sweeter around the corner.

Do something silly. Play a game with your family members or with your pets. Watch a funny movie. Find a way to laugh and raise your vibration. Once you LET GO and really laugh hard, you will feel lighter. This lighter feeling you are experiencing is your vibration rising to the level at which it was designed to be.

As your vibration rises, you will feel your energy blossom and grow because your light shines brighter. Your feelings of self-love, confidence, and well-being will create a desire to love others and the world around you. You will find yourself doing more and more random acts of kindness. You may feel forgiveness for the people who have caused you deep pain and your resentment will drift away as you begin to see them as loving spirits on a journey. Tune into your ability to raise your vibration and start enjoying the results of operating at a higher frequency.

Lesson 24:

People Are Pages—
You Are the Author of Your Life Story

Mind/Body Preparation: *Before we proceed, let's take three deep, cleansing breaths. Relax all muscles and unclench your jaw. Allow your breath to blow away any stress. Keep your breathing slow and even. On your next breath and before you close your eyes, take this thought with you: "People come and go."*

• • • • •

Meditation identifies the temporary roles others can play in our life. It shows that, just like in a story, people sometimes move on and we encounter new relationships around the corner.

As you continue in daily meditation, you may gradually feel yourself looking at life a little differently. You may discover truths about yourself that you knew existed but had forgotten—truths that reveal your beautiful character, your personality, and your unique qualities. This is your road to bliss and a healthy ego. Validate every discovery and believe it. Don't worry about past mistakes, past regrets, or harmful words put upon you by others. THIS IS NOW, today, and this is your journey. You wake each day and open your eyes, knowing you are a beautiful light energy that can shine a little brighter.

If you were to imagine your life as one big story, what would it look like? Imagine sitting on a table in your home, a huge book that contains your life story from day one. You open the cover and see photos of yourself as a baby and written on the pages are descriptions all about YOU. When you turn the pages there are more and more stories describing all of the events that have led up to where you are in your life today. Can you see that your life is a story and that you are living in the current chapter? This is your book, your life, and all of the events—good and bad—make up your story.

From time to time I find myself daydreaming about the people that I have met along the way. Many have come and gone. It seems they appeared for a time and have now moved on. Think of some people in your own life story. They could be co-workers, friends, relatives, teachers, or even old lovers. Can you see them as pages in your book? And what about your role—can you see that you play an integral part in chapters of their books?

I grew up in a small town. There were a few families on the block but very few children around my age. One day a moving van pulled into the driveway of a nearby house. Curious, I hopped on my bike and hurried beside the small crowd of other children beginning to gather. We all stood in silence, watching and hoping for any signs that would indicate if there were any kids in this family. The driver pulled open the back of the truck and there before our eyes were several bikes! My heart jumped for joy, as I knew there was hope of meeting a new kid. There turned out to be five children in this family—three girls and two boys. The child closest to my age was the oldest boy. We were both around eight when he moved next door and we immediately hit it off. We built forts, climbed trees, tossed the football, and rode our bikes around town. My favorite times with him were spent shooting basketballs until dusk. We would play, just the two of us, for hours, laughing at silly games we made up. I can still remember his voice as it was cracking in those days and he was quickly growing taller.

As the years passed and we grew older we attended different high schools and drifted apart. Life moved on and we never really kept in touch. Sadly he became ill and died very young, leaving a wife and children behind. It was while attending his funeral that I met his daughters. I introduced myself to them. They were crying and sort of nodded as they shook my hand. "Your dad was a great basketball player," I said. The girls stopped crying and looked at each other.

"What?" they asked in unison. "He was?"

"Oh yes, he was quite amazing. I have many fond memories of him beating me at every game." They had never known this about their father and encouraged me to tell them all about those childhood days. Their dad, my childhood friend, was a chapter in my book that I was happy to talk about. Sharing that chapter with his daughters somehow lightened their grief, if only momentarily.

There are many characters in your book. They may take on various roles, such as supportive cast members or destructive troublemakers. They come in various ages, races, and sexes. Take a look at your life and see these people as pages.

For many years I attended religious institutions. I made many friends and spent vacations, celebrations, and many social events centered around a few of the members I called my "friends." Some of these people took up almost twenty years in my pages. We laughed and cried together and I assumed they would stick by me through good times and bad. I was moving through these events with a smile on my face, while crying myself to sleep each night in an unhappy marriage. I didn't reveal this to anyone, since they were also friends with my spouse and I felt it wouldn't be fair to speak about my divorce plans. Should I have? Probably, but I chose to continue playing the part of the happy couple in order to make everyone else feel happy. When I began to pull away from the church, the "friends" dropped me like a hot potato. Huh? I knew that the church teaches divorce as sinful, but I had not realized that they would write me out of their next chapter. I moved on as they silently shook their disapproving heads at the poor woman who threw away her life and all of the rules of the church to find her happy place in the sun. I am just a character in their book. This is okay. That is their story and they can write it however they choose. And, as you can see, so can I.

I would be remiss if I did not address the characters in our lives who have made us feel guilty. Have you ever approached an upcoming holiday celebration with dread? Why do we continue to allow this into our lives? Carefully look at the words as defined in the Merriam-Webster Dictionary.

Celebrate: verb—to do something special or enjoyable for an important event, occasion, holiday, etc.

Dread: verb—to feel extreme reluctance to meet or face.

Do these two words even belong together in the same sentence? For years I attended a holiday meal that was a two-hour drive from my home. It did not feel like a very happy occasion to me, as I remained silent while my son, strapped into his car seat, howled. My other children grimaced in frustration, which added even more stress to our miserable commute. Every year it was the same routine. Unload the car, keep the kids from blocking the TV tuned into the non-stop golf channel, and try to help the other women in the overcrowded kitchen. Children grew tired as the adult conversation droned on and we didn't dare leave until all of the breakable, non-dishwasher-safe china was washed, dried, and tucked back into place. Yes, this was the "celebration." One year my oldest son simply refused to go. He tearfully confronted me about the farce this all had become. Finally I spoke up and ended this unhappy yearly trek. This was not an easy thing to do and it ruffled some feathers, but it was the voice of a child that helped me see it for what it was. I was engaging in a practice that was creating unhappy memories for my own children. It was just that simple step of facing something head on that allowed me to break-free and help create something much happier for everyone.

While you move through your book you may come across some individuals (even family members) who are no longer a part of your life. Recognize that they are still a part of your story, it is just that for whatever reasons either you or they have CHOSEN to remove them as daily characters. I am not advocating holding grudges. Rather, I am stating the fact that people are pages and whether they are blood related or past acquaintances they play their part in your book of life.

Have you ever met someone who struggles with a difficult family member? Do you? What part do they play in the story of your life? If you find that they cause more pain than joy, it is time to see them as characters that may need to be removed from your book. How? By limiting the time spent with these individuals. Learn to set healthy boundaries. See them as humans that are either emotionally unstable or unable to be trusted to be for your highest good. Whatever the reason—validate that you are allowing yourself to be in the line of their fire and learn to protect yourself. Don't get caught up in, "But they are my sister, my father, my Uncle." They are adults who lack the ability to be loving and kind and you are doing them no favors by enabling them to continue to hurt you. Just because they were born into your family does not give them the right to be continually vindictive. Give yourself permission to turn the page of your book and MOVE ON.

Use the tools of LETTING GO you have learned with Sæ-sii meditation and apply them to the pages of your book. Allow the positive to stay and the negative to disappear. Be aware of your own walk and understand that you are a page in the books of others. How will they write about you?

Lesson 25:

The Attitude of Gratitude—
Recognizing the Value of Appreciation

Mind/Body Preparation: *Now that we've come to our final lesson, let us revisit some of the things we have learned. If by reading this book you have started to meditate daily and intend to stick with it, excellent—you are on an amazing journey. If you find that the amount of time is too long and it keeps you from committing yourself, then shorten it to five minutes daily and work your way up to fifteen minutes. It is important that you make this work for you. Your goal is not how long; it is about being consistent, incorporating Sæ-sii meditation into your daily routine. Remember, be honest with yourself—you are making a commitment to self because YOU DESERVE THIS.*

• • • • •

Meditation opens the door to self-love and sincere gratitude for the happiness that comes with it.

In the opening lesson of this book we learned that this daily meditation is your linking-up time. You are not waiting or doing anything. You are simply sitting in silence and allowing your ability to NOT THINK happen in order to have a clean slate for information to be brought TO you. Moments of inspiring thoughts may actually occur NOT during the meditation but while you are doing something else. When a remarkable realization reveals itself you'll want to do something with this inspiration. This is the only DOING part of the meditation—following this inspiring thought and actually creating with it. How? By understanding that you have had this ability all along and that perhaps negativity, self-doubt, or just time-management has kept you from bringing it to fruition. Meditation helped unlock it and brought it to you. This is just one of the reasons why you meditate.

Some students have told me about the pitfalls that prevent them from setting aside the time to meditate. It is as if they want ME to click my fingers and create something magical for them. You've heard the old saying—you reap what you sow. It's the same with Sæ-sii meditation. You AND I, because this is the simple truth, are each a WORK IN PROGRESS. Just as I am developing at a pace designed especially for me, YOU are developing at your own rate.

If you still feel you are unable to sit in silence, then try doing this in the shower as the water falls over you. Imagine it washing away all stress. You can also meditate while taking a walk. Just let your mind float into that daydreaming state. Perhaps you can take a relaxing bike ride and simply zone out. It isn't important how you LET GO of thought, only that you do it. Find the method that works for you.

Sæ-sii meditation was taught to me by Mick and Sylvie Avery, a husband and wife team living in the U. K. who have written several spiritual books. I am eternally grateful for learning this method of silent meditation as it continues to bring me good health. I lovingly pass this along to all of my readers and acknowledge this as a wonderful gift I have learned through Mick and Sylvie's excellent teachings. Giving thanks seems like such a small thing but in reality it is bathed in loving thoughts and these thoughts will land and penetrate the heart.

Each time we close a meditation we close in a state of thankfulness. Much like your positive affirmations that we opened each lesson with, these closing remarks help show appreciation to your higher self. Sæ-sii meditation is a commitment you have made to YOU. By closing this special time in gratitude you are validating the importance of what this simple daily exercise has brought you—one step closer to finding your bliss.

Carry this attitude with you throughout your day. When you are busy with a task and a moment of inspiration filters in and lights up your life, pause and give thanks. This is your spirit bringing you a gift.

Be thankful and accept this loving thought placed before you and spread that love to all you meet.

As We Close…

You now have all of the tools and you know exactly how to proceed. Always remember Sæ-sii meditation is a lifelong practice and you are a work in progress. Every step in this book is a guideline bought to you THROUGH meditation.

Recap:
1. Open with an invocation and set your intention. (Please refer back to page 2.) Setting your intention in your opening invocation allows you to move forward with purpose.
2. Sit in silence. Sitting in silence without waiting for anything, is helping you unclutter your mind and will give it room for positive loving energy to be brought TO you.
3. Close with a thankful heart. Closing with gratitude allows you to walk with an attitude of infinite possibilities. You are never alone and have many helpers.

Your daily practice of Sæ-sii meditation will fill you with an awakening that you never thought possible, leaving you free to do what you have always wanted to do…follow your bliss.

Guided Meditations

I have included a few meditations for you to record in your own voice. You will need a smartphone, tablet, or other recording device. Read them over once to familiarize yourself with the words before you actually hit the record button. Find a quiet space and slowly read the meditations into the microphone. Give some space between the lines and remember—don't rush it. You are using this to slowly relax yourself into a quiet, floating silence. Use these recordings from time to time to help you relax deeper into meditation.

· · · · ·

White Light of Love Guided Meditation

Sink down into your space and close your eyes.

Sit comfortably into your chair and feel your feet on the ground.

Imagine your feet as if they have roots and they begin to sink deep into the earth, grounding you.

Now, begin your slow circle-breathing. In and out, in and out.

That's good. Continue with this and just let your body sink deeper into your seat.

Breathe slowly in to the count of six and out to the count of six, relaxing more with each exhale.

On your next breath relax a little deeper and feel your body release stress on the exhale.

Continue breathing nice and slow in and out, in and out.

Now imagine a beautiful white shimmering light directly above your head.

This light is a loving energy that comes closer and closer over the very center of you.

Feel this shining white light getting slightly warmer as it comes even closer.

It is a powerful white light directly over you.

As you breathe, feel the white light as it connects with you.

This shimmering white light comes to bring healing and relaxation.

Slowly this white light falls over your head and you feel yourself relaxing even deeper.

Feel the white light as it moves down over you and you feel your eyes relax.

Now it continues down your face and you feel your ears, nose, cheeks relax.

You feel the white shimmering light move slowly down and you relax and unclench your jaw.

The light is moving through you and washing a loving, healing energy into every cell.

Feel yourself relaxing deeper and deeper into your seat.

Feel your neck and shoulders relax and release any tension.

The light flows down your torso and relaxes you even more and you just sink down a little deeper.

This light knows where to go and helps release all tension filling you with positive energy.

It's cleansing and healing every molecule as it relaxes your stomach and abdomen and down over your tailbone and your bottom.

Now it flows over your thighs and you can feel this beautiful white light cascading down over your knees and spreading relaxation over your calves. Your muscles are loose and you are feeling completely relaxed.

The white light continues to remove all stress and you are feeling calm.

Feel the white light as it moves past your ankles and begins to pool around you.

This beautiful, shimmering white light of pure love slowly rises back to the crown of your head and begins to fall like a waterfall once again over you, bringing you a sense of love and well being.

Continue in this natural slow breathing, in and out, as it brings peace beyond all understanding.

Stay in this energy and feel this white healing, relaxing light.

You will stay here for the amount of time designed exactly for you. There is no clock, no limits.

This is your white light of love.

Rainbow of Bliss Guided Meditation

The following meditation is intended to strengthen and balance your energy centers also known as chakras.

Sink down into your space and close your eyes.

Sit comfortably into your chair and feel your feet on the ground.

Imagine your feet as if they have roots and they begin to sink deep into the earth…grounding you.

Now, begin your slow circle-breathing. In and out, in and out.

Relax deeper into your seat and continue to breathe slowly in and out.

Imagine that every breath is inhaling positive energy and releasing all of the negative.

You are a beautiful vibrating ball of energy that lives in your physical body.

Feel your energy relaxing with every breath, your body becomes weightless as you drift.

Now imagine a beautiful shimmering white light shining directly above you.

Breathe slowly in and out, in and out. Good.

Feel the white light as it cascades down over your body relaxing you deeper into your seat.

This shimmering white light comes to bring healing and relaxation.

Slowly this white light falls over your head and you feel yourself relaxing even deeper.

Allow the light to swirl inside of you and seek out any tension.

Imagine it releases all stress and brings a cleansing healing sensation as it travels through you.

This white light knows you very well and it washes you with an intense feeling of self love.

It makes you feel special, filled with worth and gratitude for the energy being you are.

The light continues to relax every part of you moving slowly down your body like a scanner.

Feel yourself letting go of any feelings of stress as you relax deeper and deeper.

Now imagine the white light swirling and circling you like a huge protective bubble.

You are encased in this shimmering white light of loving energy and you feel completely at ease.

Now move your focus to the base of your spine in the tailbone area and visualize a vibrant red glowing ball of light.

This energy center brings health, security and vitality. It is the red root center.

Feel it empower you as it connects you to energy of the earth.

You're radiating power and the red light strengthens your ability to get up and go. This is the center that focuses on fight or flight.

You are rooted to the Earth and this center reminds you of this grounded connection and the strength it brings you whenever you call upon it.

Breathe the color red in and out and see yourself at peace with your ability to take care of yourself.

Allow this red spinning ball of light to strengthen your survival skills.

Relax into the sensation of feeling you have the power to meet all of your needs.

Sink into your comfort zone feeling warm, safe and rested.

Feel yourself healthier than you've ever felt before.

Now let this vibrant red light continue to glow and spin as you move up to your next energy center, located about two inches below your navel.

Here, see a radiant glowing orange ball of light. This orange ball holds the energy of finances, desires, passion, sexuality and creativity.

You feel this as the pit of your stomach; this is where things affect you.

Your gut instincts are centered here and are supported by this orange light.

Breathe in this vibrant orange color and feel it bring the gifts of being content, enthusiastic, sexually fulfilled, prosperous and satisfied.

See yourself experiencing a treasure of wealth in all areas, being grateful for the abundance in your life now, and imagine riches flowing to you like a river.

They come from expected and unexpected babbling brooks running straight to you.

Let this orange ball continue to glow and spin as you move up to your next energy center located a few inches above your navel.

This is the solar plexus energy center. Here, see a beautiful sunny yellow glowing ball of light.

As you breathe in a shimmering yellow color, feel it expand your joy, self-esteem, and will power.

See yourself successful and deeply fulfilled in whatever you choose to create.

It is this bright yellow light that can ignite and fire your passions and create action moving you toward your higher purpose.

This is the area that helps you move with your passion of purpose.

Feel the glowing yellow energy empower you as you move up to your next energy center at the middle of your chest, and visualize a beautiful emerald green glowing ball of light.

This is your heart energy. This is the light of love for yourself and others.

This glowing green ball of light fills you with inner peace.

A loving green energy that can get to-the-heart-of-the-matter quickly, it swells with each breath you take.

Let it glow, bringing compassion, self-acceptance, and the ability to love deeply and unconditionally.

Breathe in this green shimmering ball of light and let these feelings grow even larger, seeing yourself living in perfect harmony and acceptance with everyone in your life.

Be filled with gratitude for all that has been provided for you.

Feel your heart opening and expanding with compassion and forgiveness for yourself and others.

Now let this heart energy continue to shimmer and spin and gently move up to another energy center located at your throat, visualizing a beautiful blue color.

This beautiful blue ball of light is the gateway between the body and mind. It helps you transmit and receive information.

A blue glowing light that enables you to listen to the vibrations and sounds that bring clarity.

This energy enables you to communicate with truth and wisdom and express yourself with confidence.

Breathe this blue energy in and out, see yourself happily expressing yourself through creativity.

Let this light encompass whatever creative gifts you enjoy such as singing, writing, painting, dancing, playing a sport, anything you do for fun.

Let this brilliant blue ball of energy continue to glow and spin and gently move up to your next energy center located at the middle of your forehead.

See a beautiful deep mixture of purple and blue light. It is an indigo blue glowing ball of light and it knows you very well.

As it glows it expands your imagination, psychic abilities, inner knowing and wisdom.

This indigo blue shimmering light expands with every breath and helps you see the synergies along your path.

It enables you to follow the road signs that appear as if out of the blue, guiding you step by step.

Feel this indigo blue ball spinning and raising your awareness of your sixth sense and feel your perception deepen as it opens wider to bring a brilliance that is waiting for you to unlock.

This light brings trust in knowing you do not need to explain yourself to your higher power.

Your subconscious and conscious selves work in harmony for your highest good.

Now let this indigo light continue to glow and spin as you gently move up to your crown energy center at the top of your head.

See a beautiful violet ball of radiating light spinning at the very top of your head. This is the energy of spirituality, thought, and service to others.

Breathe in violet and let this light glow as it brings gifts of self-knowledge, spiritual connection and bliss.

As this light expands allow it to bring amazing "aha moments" and liberation as it takes you to a place of infinite possibilities.

See yourself living in wisdom and awareness, blending with a sacred love, a love that allows you to be of service to all things including mankind, plants, minerals and animals.

Let this violet ball of shimmering light glow and spin as you bring your awareness back to the white bubble of protective light that encircles you.

Now slowly breathe this beautiful white light in through your top of your head down into all of the spinning colors of light that make up your energy centers.

Breathe in the white light down through the violet at the top of your crown and slowly down to the indigo located at your brow.

Now down through the blue at your throat, pull it down through the green at your heart, even further down through the yellow at your middle, and down through the orange just below your navel, and all the way down to your red light at the base of your spine.

Now breathe the white light back up the way it came.

As it passes through each center bring a small light beam of each color all the way up to the top of your head.

See all of these colors spinning and mixing at the crown of your head.

Now visualize the red, orange, yellow, green, blue, indigo and violet lights creating a beam of combined energy—shooting out the top of your head directly into the universe.

Feel your connection to the Universe and allow yourself to be one with it.

Stay in this beautiful space for as long as you wish.

Continue to breathe slowly in and out knowing that every molecule in your body is helping you find your bliss.

You are a living, breathing ball of energy filled with LOVE. You ARE loved.

"We must all understand that life holds a lot of broken bits and pieces. We have storms and trials and sometimes fall flat on our face. It is how we are able to create something from this that will enable us to love ourselves more. It will help us to feel complete, whole and beautiful and allow us to soar."

— Lorraine Turner and Guides

To learn more about Lorraine, please visit calicohorses.com or email info@calicohorses.com

CPSIA information can be obtained
at www.ICGtesting.com
Printed in the USA
LVHW050200081019
633409LV00001B/327/P